SKETCHNOTING IN THE CLASSROOM

A Practical Guide to Deepen Student Learning

NICHOLE CARTER

International Society for Technology in Education
PORTLAND, OREGON • ARLINGTON, VIRGINIA

Dedication

TO MY FAMILY; BRIAN, MOLLY, BRAD, AND NANCY, THANK YOU FOR YOUR SUPPORT AND GUIDANCE ON THIS PROJECT. BRAD AND NANCY, THANK YOU FOR INSTILLING IN ME A HARD-WORK ETHIC AND THE POWER TO BELIEVE IN MYSELF. BRIAN AND MOLLY, YOU GUYS ARE THE REASON I WORK SO HARD. I AM PRETTY PROUD OF THIS, AND I HOPE YOU ARE TOO.

Sketchnoting in the Classroom

A Practical Guide to Deepen Student Learning

Nichole Carter

SENIOR ACQUISITIONS EDITOR: Valerie Witte
DEVELOPMENTAL AND COPY EDITOR: Linda Laflamme
PROOFREADER: Steffi Drewes
INDEXER: Valerie Haynes Perry
BOOK DESIGN AND PRODUCTION: Danielle Foster
COVER DESIGN: Edwin Ouellette

LIBRARY OF CONGRESS CATALOGING-IN-PUBLICATION DATA

Names: Carter, Nichole, author.

Title: Sketchnoting in the classroom : a practical guide to deepen student learning / Nichole Carter.

Description: First edition. | Portland, Oregon : International Society for Technology in Education, [2019] | Includes bibliographical references and index.

Identifiers: LCCN 2019010653 (print) | LCCN 2019021881 (ebook) | ISBN 9781564847751 (ePub) | ISBN 9781564847744 (mobi) | ISBN 9781564847768 (pdf) | ISBN 9781564847775 (pbk. : alk. paper)

Subjects: LCSH: Sketchnoting.

Classification: LCC LB2395.25 (ebook) | LCC LB2395.25 .C3745 2019 (print) | DDC 371.302/81--dc23

LC record available at https://lccn.loc.gov/2019010653

FIRST EDITION

ISBN: 978-1-56484-777-5

Ebook version available

Printed in the United States of America

ISTE® is a registered trademark of the International Society for Technology in Education

ABOUT ISTE

The International Society for Technology in Education (ISTE) is a nonprofit organization that works with the global education community to accelerate the use of technology to solve tough problems and inspire innovation. Our worldwide network believes in the potential technology holds to transform teaching and learning.

ISTE sets a bold vision for education transformation through the ISTE Standards, a framework for students, educators, administrators, coaches and computer science educators to rethink education and create innovative learning environments. ISTE hosts the annual ISTE Conference & Expo, one of the world's most influential edtech events. The organization's professional learning offerings include online courses, professional networks, year-round academies, peer-reviewed journals and other publications. ISTE is also the leading publisher of books focused on technology in education. For more information or to become an ISTE member, visit iste.org. Subscribe to ISTE's YouTube channel and connect with ISTE on Twitter, Facebook and LinkedIn.

Related ISTE Titles

Stretch Yourself: A Personalized Journey to Deepen Your Teaching Practice

Caitlin McLemore and Fanny Passeport

To see all books available from ISTE, please visit iste.org/resources.

ABOUT THE AUTHOR

 Nichole Carter has been in education since 2004. She has taught everything from geography to U.S. history to reading intervention to eighth-grade English. After teaching English with a ton of tech integration, Nichole changed districts and has been an innovation strategist working with K–12 classrooms on all things instructionally innovative.

In 2015, Nichole decided to start researching how to sketchnote. After trying it for awhile herself, she proceeded to train her district's entire multilingual department of 220 educators, and then began teaching an introductory class. To date, she has taught more than 100 sessions on sketchnoting in education.

Professionally and personally, Nichole believes in the power of creating, whether it is sketchnotes, art, videos, or even a great plate of pasta. Inspiring other people to create and make is a big part of her educational pedagogy.

Nichole lives with her husband Brian, her daughter Molly, and two Wheaten Terriers (Winston and Stewart), just outside of Portland, Oregon. She loves reading, music, cooking, and creating art.

For resources on sketchnoting and more, visit her at mrscarterhla.com.

ACKNOWLEDGMENTS

Jon Samuelson, thank you for always being willing to give me advice and to reach out to your vast network to find me answers when we couldn't figure it out on our own. I value your advice.

Jon Peplinski, thank you for being a great leader, for encouraging me to pursue something I was interested in, and giving me the materials to get started.

Nancy Anderson, thank you for helping me through the initial stages and guidance through the book contract phase. You helped me "lean in" and know my worth.

Valerie Witte, thank you for approaching me to write this book, pitching it to your team, and being patient with my silly questions and anxious to-do lists.

Linda Laflamme, thank you so much for being such a great editor. I knew that when I put my thoughts on the page that you would come back through with guidance and a perspective that always made sense. I appreciate the process with you.

Danielle Foster, thank you for taking my rough draft and making it a reality. I know I didn't always understand the process, but thank you for staying with me.

Featured Classroom Voices: Leah LaCrosse, Bettina Curl, Heather Hoxie, Cynthia Nixon, Misty Kluesner, Manuel Herrera, thank you for your support, contributions, and help through this process. You are amazing educators and I am so glad to call you friends and colleagues.

Teammates, thank you for your support and your interest in how the process was going for me. I appreciated any and all guidance and support during the creation of my first solo book.

CONTENTS

WHO IS THIS BOOK FOR?   XI

HOW TO USE THIS BOOK   XI

SECTION I: THE WHAT & WHY OF SKETCHNOTES

CHAPTER 1   SKETCHNOTE BEGINNINGS   **4**

The History of Modern Sketchnotes   5

Yes, You Can Draw!   8

Let's Play a Doodle Game   9

CHAPTER 2   THE BRAIN RESEARCH BEHIND SKETCHNOTES   **14**

Building Your Visual Vocabulary   15

Dual Coding Theory   17

Temple Grandin   21

CHAPTER 3 STANDARDS, METACOGNITION
& FOCUS 22

ISTE, NCTE & Common Core Standards 24

Metacognition 29

Drawing Break: How to Make Toast 30

Focus & Categorization or Synthesis 32

CHAPTER 4 INTRODUCING SKETCHNOTES
IN A CLASS 34

Visual Vocabulary 36

Sketchnote Structure 44

Implementation of Sketchnote Basics 53

CHAPTER 5 ANALOG VERSUS DIGITAL 54

Exploring Sketchnoting Styles 55

Analog Tools 57

Digital Tools 59

Analog versus Digital Quiz 64

CHAPTER 6 REAL-TIME VERSUS REVISITED
STRATEGIES 66

Which Version Should You Start with in Class? 68

Listening Comprehension Strategies 69

Strategies to Build Speed During Real-Time
Sketchnotes   72

The Four Cs of 21st Century Learning   74

SECTION II: SKETCHNOTES ACROSS CONTENT AREAS

CHAPTER 7 SKETCHNOTES IN SCIENCE CLASS **82**

Lab Write-Ups   83

Lab Rules   87

End-of-Unit Review   88

CHAPTER 8 SKETCHNOTES IN SOCIAL STUDIES **92**

Current Events   94

Timelines   99

Cause & Effect   101

Sketchnotes During Speeches   101

CHAPTER 9 SKETCHNOTES IN ELA **106**

Sketchnote a Plotline of a Story   108

Readers & Writers Workshop (Mini-Lessons)   111

Podcasts   113

Read-Alouds   114

Journal Prompts   115

CHAPTER 10 SKETCHNOTES IN MATH 120

Sketchnote a Story Problem 124

Vocab Review 129

Explain a Formula or Current Content 130

CHAPTER 11 ASSESSMENT & EVALUATION 134

Setting Up Students for Success 135

Quick Grading Tips & Tricks 137

Feedback from Structure & Partner Work 139

JOIN AN ONLINE COMMUNITY 142

Online Challenges & Prompts 143

People to Follow 149

Go Practice Sketchnotes 149

REFERENCES 152

INDEX 160

ONLINE ONLY

BONUS CHAPTER 12: SKETCHNOTES IN PROJECT DESIGN

BONUS CHAPTER 13: SKETCHNOTES FOR YOUR OWN PROFESSIONAL DEVELOPMENT

BONUS APPENDIX A: MORE HOW-TO SKETCHES TO GET STARTED

BONUS APPENDIX B: GLOSSARY

WHO IS THIS BOOK FOR ?

This is a book for educators, educators that strive to give all the tools possible to their students to be successful in their learning. Sketchnotes are a form of note taking and as such work great for students in grades 3–12. Sketchnotes aren't about making art in its truest sense; they are about learning and retention. This book is about tapping into something that our brains are inherently used to. So, if you are sitting there thinking, "I can't draw," have no fear: By the end of this book, I will give you the tools to feel successful on starting your journey of visual note taking.

HOW TO USE THIS BOOK :

This book is meant to be marked up, drawn on, doodled in, and actively participated with. Please draw in any of the blank spaces, and try out the activities as you go. You will find QR codes to scan along the way for additional content. Plus, the book's companion website is packed with two bonus chapters, tutorial videos, how-to drawings, monthly challenges and prompts to keep you going, as well as lesson plans.

Website Password

Sketch19

THE WHAT & WHY OF SKETCHNOTES

CHAPTER 1   Sketchnote Beginnings

CHAPTER 2   The Brain Research Behind Sketchnotes

CHAPTER 3   Standards, Metacognition & Focus

CHAPTER 4   Introducing Sketchnotes in a Class

CHAPTER 5   Analog versus Digital

CHAPTER 6   Real-Time versus Revisited Strategies

CHAPTER 1

SKETCHNOTE BEGINNINGS

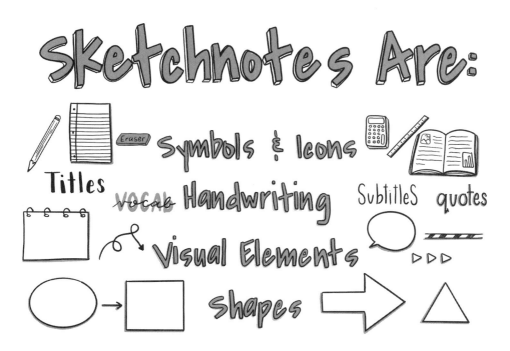

Sketchnotes Are:

Titles · Symbols & Icons · VOCAB · Handwriting · Subtitles · quotes · Visual Elements · Shapes

Sketchnotes are a form of note taking. What is special about sketchnoting is that it teaches the best forms of strategic note taking, listening comprehension, synthesis, Dual Coding Theory, and note hierarchy. Plus, it allows note takers to personalize the experience based on their own past knowledge and, to some extent, their emotional connection to the new information they are learning.

The History of Modern Sketchnotes

Although the story of modern sketchnotes and graphic recording can be traced back at least fifty years ago, in reality people have been telling stories and making connections with images since the cave drawings of Sulawesi, Indonesia, over 35,400 years ago. Despite this common ancestry, sketchnotes and graphic recording have definite differences.

Sketchnotes and visual note taking are similar in definition, and educators have been using visuals for decades, especially in relation to language acquisition. The word *sketchnotes* can be traced back to Mike Rohde and 2007; since then, the practice of sketchnoting, whether in a digital or analog form, has taken off. Sketchnotes for professional development and their use in education can be traced back to 2013, when Sylvia Duckworth, an educator from Toronto, began sketchnoting edtech buzzwords and pedagogy.

30,000 years ago rock/cave paintings

1970s board meetings

2007 Mike Rohde coined word sketchnotes

2013 Sylvia Duckworth begins edu-sketching

Currently 5th wave of graphic recording

Graphic recording, however, can be traced back to the 1970s when visual facilitation experts could be seen popping up in board meetings. We are currently in the fifth or sixth wave of graphic recording. Today, for example, *Fortune 500* companies ask graphic recording artists to record and make sense of their planning meetings. Graphic recording is much more difficult than sketchnoting, as it requires not just listening comprehension but the ability to make your notes consumable for others. With sketchnotes, the audience is you; it is a form of note taking that sticks, because it is unique and personal to you. For instance, this is how I would draw a sketchnote on what I learned about the differences between sketchnotes and graphic recording.

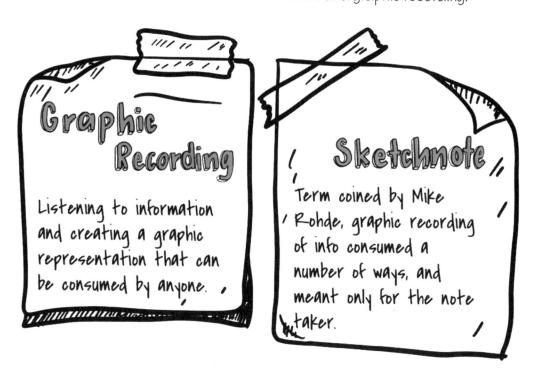

Graphic Recording

Listening to information and creating a graphic representation that can be consumed by anyone.

Sketchnote

Term coined by Mike Rohde, graphic recording of info consumed a number of ways, and meant only for the note taker.

Yes, You Can Draw!

If you are looking at some of my sketchnotes already and comparing your first attempts, please don't. Sketchnoting takes practice, and that is what this book is all about. One of the things that I hear the most from adults, and students over the age of twelve, is that they can't draw.

By the time we reach middle school, many of us have identified ourselves as artistic or just not. In this book, we are going to let go of those preconceived notions and judgments. Moving forward you are a sketchnoter. You are taking the first steps to have the skill set to make this easier and easier for your brain and your artistic abilities!

 Scan the QR code for Graham Shaw's TEDx Talk, "Why People Believe They Can't Draw." Get out a pen and paper or a digital device, and draw along with him.

You can't pick up a pencil and expect to draw the *Mona Lisa* on the first go; you have to practice. As my friend and colleague Carrie Baughcum (@HeckAwesome), a fellow sketchnoter, likes to say, "It's not a sprint, it's a marathon." She's right: You get better and better the more you train. The more you ask your brain to conjure up images or symbols, the easier it becomes. To prove it, jump-start your brain with a little game.

Let's Play A

DOODLE GAME

Build Your Visual Vocabulary With

GRAPHIC

JAM

Draw an icon or image for each of the words in the bottom-left corner. Time yourself, allowing about 10 seconds to just draw, before moving to the next word.

Book
Backpack
School Lunch
Report
School

Scan here to get a 10-second timer!

What is interesting about this activity (which was inspired by a similar one in Sunni Brown's *The Doodle Revolution*) is that our brains can come up with different icons and images for the same word. This makes our notes unique to us, thus helping with the retention. For example, when I introduce sketchnoting to a class— of educators or students— I always ask them to draw the word *cup*. Some will draw a water cup, and some will draw a coffee or tea cup. When I ask people how they might draw a phone, students automatically think of the iconic iPhone, which is much easier to draw. Adults typically think of a rotary phone and attempt to draw that, which is obviously much more difficult. Sometimes age and life experiences can influence your thought process.

In the space provided draw a cup and a phone.

This difference of perspective is again what makes sketchnotes so important: They are unique to you. Giving your brain freedom of expression in that manner is a skill to practice. Try it now: Draw a symbol or icon for the word *life*.

SKETCHNOTE BEGINNINGS

A great way to continue your practice, or provide some for your students, is to check out the book's companion site for Chapter 1 to find a list of school-related icons to draw.

Another option is to try Google Quick, Draw! With this online game, you draw the suggested word, while Google AI tries to guess what you are drawing! To try Google Quick, Draw!, scan the QR code.

CHAPTER 2

THE BRAIN RESEARCH BEHIND SKETCHNOTES

Brains love the ability to practice and build their muscle memory. We call this building

YOUR VISUAL VOCABULARY

Brains also love visuals, and they need connections for what they learn. The more connections, the deeper the learning.

If we deliver information in only one specific way, we are neglecting other brain functions. When we teach the skill of reading, we know that in order for the brain to comprehend the text many different connections and areas of the brain have to be functioning. Sketchnotes ask the brain to interact in a multisensory and multimodal learning way, similarly to reading. Considering this, shouldn't we give more priority to the act of note taking in our current curriculum?

visual

Auditory

Kinesthetic

We know that learners come in different shapes and sizes; a one-size-fits-all approach to note taking doesn't work any more than a one-size-fits-all approach to reading does. We need to give students the tools they need to be successful.

We need to offer more time in the classroom for these multisensory and multimodal learning activities. Sketchnotes are an easy way to do just that!

Sketchnoting also taps into Dual Coding Theory. Often discussed by multilingual teachers, Dual Coding Theory is the idea that when you are acquiring new language content, attaching an image to the verbal content can help you retain that information more.

75% of our entire sensory processing capacity is dedicated to vision.

Images are processed 60,000 times faster than text.

Images are processed simultaneously and text is processed sequentially. This is why "glance media" asks whether your message can be processed effectively within 3 seconds.

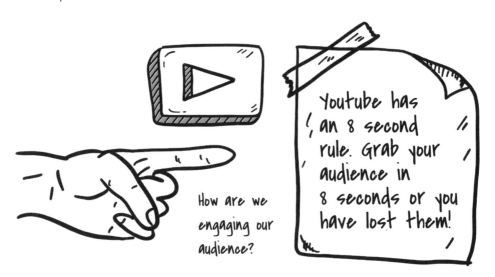

How are we engaging our audience?

Youtube has an 8 second rule. Grab your audience in 8 seconds or you have lost them!

When touch is combined with vision, learning jumps by 30%

Even for students who are able to take great regular notes, sketchnoting, or drawing images to represent those concepts, helps them more deeply understand the content.

You are extracting the passivity of even the most well-written notes, because sketchnoting demands active processing and recall.

People remember only 10% of what they hear, 20% of what they read, 80% of what they see and do.

A great personal example of thinking in pictures, Temple Grandin figured out at a young age that her brain worked differently from the people around her. This sketchnote of Temple's story was inspired by her picture book, which would be excellent for introducing the subject of sketchnoting in the younger grades. The QR code on the next page can lead you to a few articles that would be great in secondary classes.

TEMPLE GRANDIN

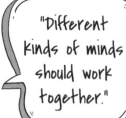

"Different kinds of minds should work together."

NOTE

Dr. Temple Grandin, a professor of animal science, often says "I am different not less." to describe her feelings about life with autism. She wrote a book about how she thinks in pictures. The picture book The Girl Who Thought in Pictures would be a great resource to introduce sketchnotes in the 3rd to 5th grade classrooms.

"I used to think stupidity was the cause of people not being able to see things that were obvious to me. Today I realize it was not stupidity; it is just a different way of thinking."

Scan the QR code for more from Temple Grandin. This could be used in the secondary classroom or for your own knowledge.

@MRSCARTERHLA

Temple Grandin realized she thought in pictures and began to use that to her advantage. Sketchnoting is another tool for students to use to their advantage, and, as you can see, it is a very powerful tool for the brain.

CHAPTER 3

STANDARDS, METACOGNITION & FOCUS

So we know that attaching images to our connections in new learning is good for our brain, but how does it fit into the curriculum? Although parts of sketchnotes can be taught at younger ages, the act of note taking doesn't appear in Common Core State Standards until third grade. The process of sketchnotes engages students while reinforcing summary and synthesis. To start this kind of focused note taking at third grade and potentially carry it forward would be great for most students. Depending on how you introduce sketchnotes, and model them for your students, you could not only fulfill International Society for Technology in Education (ISTE) Standards, Common Core State Standards, and National Council of Teachers of English (NCTE) standards, but also potentially prompt them to really start thinking about their thinking.

Note Taking Standards

How do you currently teach note taking in your classroom? Draw a quick sketchnote about what questions you have about this process. Or what actions you are hoping to take on note taking after this book.

ISTE, NCTE & Common Core Standards
ISTE Standards for Educators

STANDARDS
6 Facilitator

Educators facilitate learning with technology to support student achievement of the ISTE Standards for Students. Educators:

- 6a Foster a culture where students take ownership of their learning goals and outcomes in both independent and group settings.
- 6d Model and nuture creativity and creative expression to communicate ideas, knowledge or connections.

FACILITATOR: Teachers need to model the process of sketchnoting with their students to create a culture of acceptance; brain-based research shows that the more we offer these types of immersive multimodal learning options for students, the higher the retention rate and the more brain connections will be made. As the teacher, you must model your thinking when you choose to take sketchnotes using digital or traditional tools, directly stating your thinking process as you begin, because students must eventually make those decisions. Creating a culture where kids feel safe to doodle and draw to show their learning doesn't just happen because you state your intentions. You have to model on a regular basis, which means you should be doodling and sketchnoting with them. As Sunni Brown said in her book, *The Doodle Revolution*, "You are creating a space where students shouldn't fear making doodle-rich messes in service of generating ideas and mapping conversations."

ISTE Standards for Students

STANDARDS

3 Knowledge Constructor

Students critically curate a variety of resources using digital tools to construct knowledge, produce creative artifacts and make meaningful learning experiences for themselves and others.

- 3c Students curate information from digital resources using a variety of tools and methods to create collections of artifacts that demonstrate meaningful connections or conclusions.

- 3d Students build knowledge by actively exploring real-world issues and problems, developing ideas and theories and pursuing answers and solutions.

KNOWLEDGE CONSTRUCTOR: We need to give students the tools to be successful in note taking and study techniques, as well as support them in choosing the right tool for the job at hand. Explicit instruction in sketchnotes can help in both of those areas. If you have access to digital tools, then giving students the option to take notes with the aid of technology or paper and pencil is another step in helping them construct their own knowledge from a variety of resources. I love doing my daily planners, and teaching sketchnote basics to students in analog form. For my own personal sketchnotes, however, I prefer to go digital. By practicing in many areas and considering my thinking and learning, I figured out what I like best. We need to give students the same courtesy and opportunities to decide. We will discuss the benefits of digital and analog approaches in Chapter 5.

STANDARDS

6 Creative Communicator

Students communicate clearly and express themselves creatively for a variety of purposes using the platforms, tools, styles, formats and digital media appropriate to their goals.

- 6a Students choose the appropriate platforms and tools for meeting the desired objectives of their creation or communication.

- 6b Students create original works or responsibly repurpose or remix digital resources into new creations.

- 6c Students communicate complex ideas clearly and effectively by creating or using a variety of digital objects such as visualizations, models or simulations.

- 6d Students publish or present content that customizes the message and medium for their intended audiences.

CREATIVE COMMUNICATOR: Students need to choose how best to communicate for their learning needs. Using sketchnotes is not always for every student, but it is a great tool for ELL students and for revisiting information. Especially in an AVID classroom where Cornell notes are front and center, you can add a layer of sketchnotes when you revisit your notes. AVID is designed to help underachieving students with high academic potential prepare for college. It relies a lot on organizational skills, teaching note taking, and tutoring—good skills for students in any program. By allowing students to create sketchnotes, even as an added layer to traditional notes, you are making it easier to communicate complex ideas through symbolism that is unique to them.

NCTE Standards

STANDARDS
NCTE

- Students conduct research on issues and interests by generating ideas and questions, and by posing problems. They gather, evaluate, and synthesize data from a variety of sources to communicate their discoveries in ways that suit their purpose and audience.

- Students use a variety of technological and information resources to gather and synthesize information and to create and communicate knowledge.

- Students use spoken, written, and visual language to accomplish their own purposes.

According to NCTE standards, a student should show proficiencies in research and synthesis of information from a variety of texts, and communicate that through "spoken, written, and visual language." Although the standard doesn't explicitly mention it, note taking is a powerful step in helping students synthesize data from a variety of sources.

Common Core State Standards

STANDARDS
8 Writing

- Recall information from experiences or gather information from print and digital sources.
- Take brief notes on sources and sort evidence into provided categories.

For third grade, Common Core writing standard 8 introduces the concept of students taking notes for research papers. We see this standard continue to evolve through subsequent years to showcase how students begin to synthesize information and make connections between multiple texts.

Sketchnotes Can Help

In the end, sketchnotes will not be the summative product that educators will be using to test proficiency. Instead, they help students make connections and synthesize their learning. As the classroom facilitator of knowledge, it is your job to model your own creativity, as well as nurture creativity in your room—sketchnotes can help with that. Students need to be able to synthesize information, sometimes from multiple sources, and then communicate their knowledge in a creative way in which they choose their platform—sketchnotes can help with that. Finally, students need to be able to recall that information—sketchnotes can help with that, too!

Metacognition

A part of the conversation you need to be having with the students is about metacognition: You need to get them to stop and think about their thinking. After you have modeled a few sketchnotes and students have created several of their own sketchnotes, have students routinely dive back into their notes and look for patterns.

What icons do I use over and over again?

What feels good or is easy for me to draw, that doesn't take the focus away from what I am learning?

Do I like drawing in landscape or portrait mode?

What structure do my sketchnotes take on?

Where am I putting my title every time? Do I need to move it?

At TEDGlobal 2013, Tom Wujec spoke about problem solving through visualization and how to get people to start thinking about their thinking. To illustrate his method, he discussed what happens when he asks people to draw the process of making toast.

Drawing Break: How to Make Toast

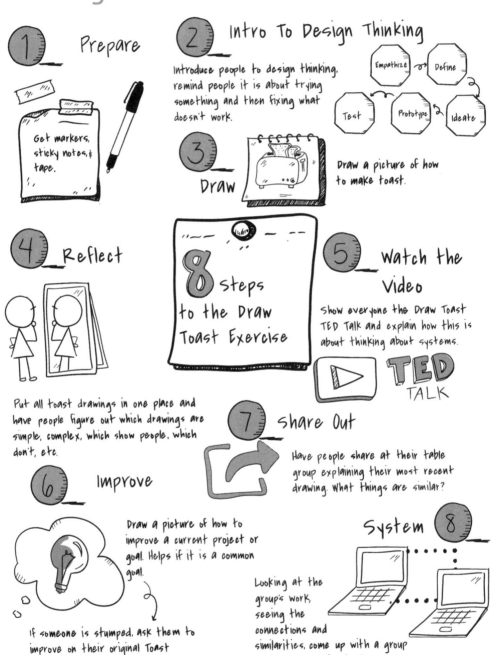

1 Prepare

Get markers, sticky notes, & tape.

2 Intro To Design Thinking

Introduce people to design thinking. remind people it is about trying something and then fixing what doesn't work.

Empathize → Define → Ideate → Prototype → Test

3 Draw

Draw a picture of how to make toast.

4 Reflect

Put all toast drawings in one place and have people figure out which drawings are simple, complex, which show people, which don't, etc.

8 Steps to the Draw Toast Exercise

5 Watch the Video

Show everyone the Draw Toast TED Talk and explain how this is about thinking about systems.

TED TALK

7 Share Out

Have people share at their table group explaining their most recent drawing. What things are similar?

6 Improve

Draw a picture of how to improve a current project or goal. Helps if it is a common goal.

If someone is stumped, ask them to improve on their original Toast drawing.

8 System

Looking at the group's work, seeing the connections and similarities, come up with a group system or solution to the goal.

STANDARDS, METACOGNITION & FOCUS

Scan the QR code to watch the Draw Toast TED Talk.

Ask your students to do the same, and you will be shocked at how many different ways they will visually describe the act of making toast. As I will discuss in more detail in the next chapter, this exercise is a great way to showcase that sketchnotes are unique to the individual and at the same time to talk about how to highlight important parts of a process. Just as an assignment to write the steps to make a peanut butter and jelly sandwich showcases the importance of word choice and sequential order, so too does this activity but through a sketchnote.

HOW TO MAKE TOAST

Use the space here to try your hand at drawing how to make toast.

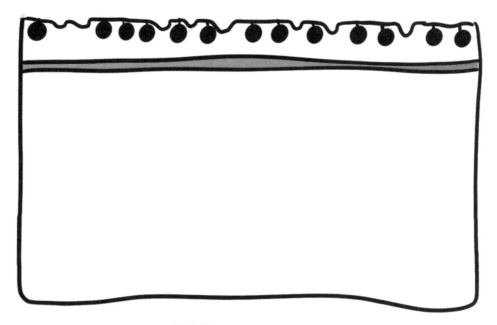

Focus & Categorization or Synthesis

When your mind and body are working in tandem, there is little room left for distractions. When students are engaged with sketchnoting, you will see their note taking accuracy increase and their listening comprehension improve. It is our natural instinct to categorize things and make connections, and sketchnotes help our brains do that. The more students practice, the easier it gets for them to make those natural connections in their brains and notes.

Nonfiction Text Features

In the next chapter, we will discuss using fonts and color in sketchnotes to emphasize hierarchy in the notes. Enhancing these skills will help students to categorize and draw attention to their connections. In addition, students will gain a better understanding of nonfiction text features as they will begin to use them with fidelity in their notes.

CHAPTER 4

INTRODUCING SKETCHNOTES IN A CLASS

This chapter is a step-by-step guide to getting started with sketchnotes in the classroom. You can choose to recreate each of the chapter's sections as 10-minute mini-lessons, or you can present the entire contents in about an hour. I'll offer more thoughts on how to convert this material for classroom use at the end of this chapter. For now, however, let's go over the basics of a sketchnote.

A Sketchnote will have:

- A title

- A mixture of text and images to convey content

- Arrows to show connections

- People (when people are mentioned in the learning)

- Containers and banners to hold important information and draw the eye

- Different types of fonts to draw the eye

Visual Vocabulary

When introducing sketchnotes to a classroom, the first thing that you must do is model and build your confidence in drawing with simple shapes. Start with the five basic elements shown below, which form the foundation of your visual vocabulary. If you can draw these, you should be able to draw any and all icons.

What you want to do is have students start to break down how to draw icons by thinking of their *visual alphabet*, the simple shapes used to create the items or symbols that make up their visual vocabulary. Even the most complex things you might have to draw in notes can be drawn in a more simple form and your brain will still recognize them. Your *visual vocabulary* is comprised of the things that you can comfortably draw right away, just like you can spell common words quickly without the help of a dictionary. For example, because I do a lot with educational technology, I am constantly drawing iPads and laptops. If I was in a science classroom my visual vocabulary would be a different set of content-related icons I could easily draw.

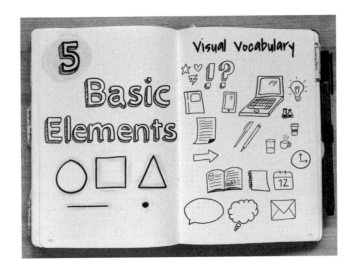

To practice using your visual alphabet and grow you visual vocabulary, try drawing the following items by combining simple shapes in the space below.

- House
- Tree
- Book
- Notebook paper

- Pencil
- Ruler
- Calculator
- Magnifying glass

Sketch here

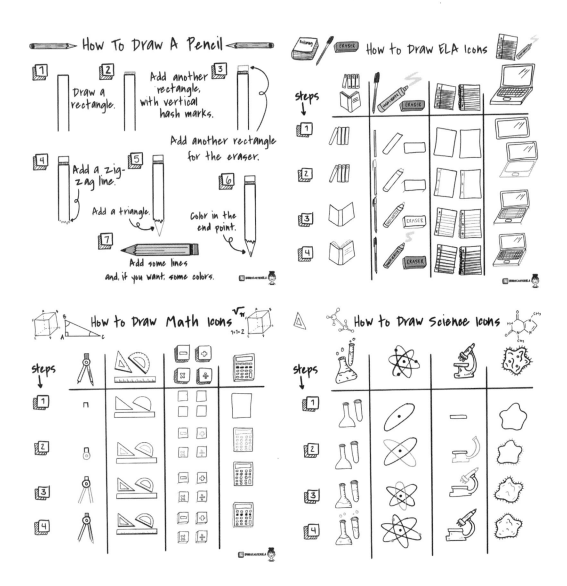

Remember, depending on how your brain interprets different words, your icons may look different from mine and your students' may look different from yours—that's okay! The important thing is that the icons are meaningful to the note taker.

Drawing People

Drawing people can be very intimidating to most people, so giving students the skills to draw people to the best of their ability is really important. We will start with filling a face matrix, which is an activity that many people practice when learning to animate faces. Minute changes in facial features can help bring about many different characters and expressions. As you look at the matrix below, you will see that each column indicates a shape to use for the eyebrows and each row indicates a mouth to combine with them.

Even shifting the mouth from the center of the face to the side or changing the shape of the head itself will give you more animation. Moving the head on the body of the person can also signify age. A head directly on top of a body with a longer space for a neck signifies youth, while less neck to no neck can show stooping and signify age.

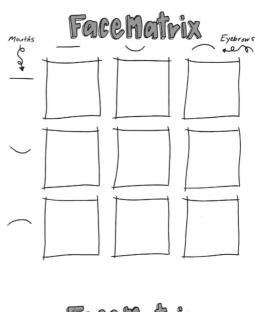

younger kids have bigger head-to-body ratio

Stooping

younger → older → oldest

old Phone → new

old (too thick)   New

try it here:

INTRODUCING SKETCHNOTES IN A CLASS

When two- and three-year-olds are first learning to hold a marker and begin drawing, they start drawing people, rather scary looking stick people, in fact.

2 Years Old: Scribbles

2-3 Years Old: Tadpole

3 Years Old: Human Figure

4-5 Years Old: Adding more accessories

4-5 Years Old: Starting to draw the world around them

4-5 Years Old: Starting to draw humans with identifying features

So third graders will have success in starting with a simple stick figure. Using the face matrix, you can easily animate a stick figure to meet the needs of your notes. When hearing or reading someone's name, good note takers will write it down. In sketchnotes, you should draw that person to help your brain better remember the name.

The Grey method allows you to start adding accessories to your stick figures. You can also denote direction by adding a simple line for a nose.

Power up Your stick Figures

Start with a stick figure.

Add extra lines and circles to animate your figure.

Hands on the hips.

When you are running one hand up and one down.

One foot on the ground and one foot in the air.

Add accessories.

Add a face from the face matrix!

Add a nose to show direction!

INTRODUCING SKETCHNOTES IN A CLASS

Another option is to think about the body shape of your people. Try using different shapes. To show age, for instance, you can use a larger circle for the head of a child and a smaller circle on a taller body for an adult.

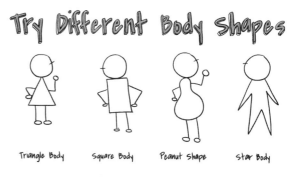

Try Different Body Shapes

Triangle Body Square Body Peanut Shape Star Body

Advanced Techniques

Some additional techniques you can try involve using shadows and hatching to imply depth and dimensionality, as well as more advanced facial features. I have even explored creating vector-style graphics by drawing over the top of a photo of an individual. You can do this using tracing paper or a drawing app that allows layering.

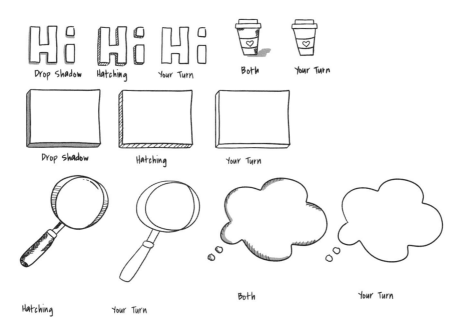

Drop Shadow   Hatching   Your Turn   Both   Your Turn

Drop Shadow   Hatching   Your Turn

Hatching   Your Turn   Both   Your Turn

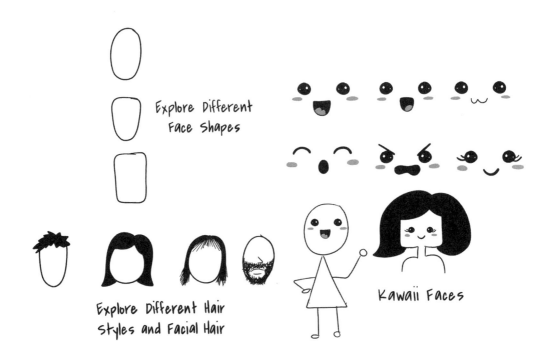

Explore Different Face Shapes

Explore Different Hair Styles and Facial Hair

Kawaii Faces

My daughter Molly

The vector-style drawing I created over her photo

Me

The drawing from over my photo

Sketchnote Structure

When I am talking with students about starting their sketchnotes, I mention that they need to think about their thinking (added bonus: prompt them with the word *metacognition*). The first question they should ask themselves is how they want to position their paper.

Do they like to draw their sketchnotes in landscape or portrait? Their answer often depends on the paper they are using too. Once they decide their paper orientation, they need to think about where they want to place their title. The placement of the title will then help them think of their structure. If their title goes at that top of the page, they will be looking at a linear, vertical, or path structure.

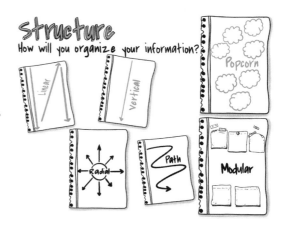

If a student decides to put the title towards the center, the most natural approach is a radial or popcorn structure. The "My Day" sketchnote here could be considered either a path (follow the arrows) or a radial (items circle the central theme) sketchnote.

If you have multiple topics to condense into one sketchnote, or multiple people speaking, you might want to separate out your page ahead of time and do a skyscraper or modular structure. These take a little bit of preplanning or knowledge on the part of the sketchnoter to break up the page into logical sections. In the classroom, you could provide this structure on a premade template for students or model it for them. The example sketchnote shows that I was listening to three brief presentations. None was long enough to really fill a whole page with notes on its own, and by grouping the speakers together in this modular structure I got more information from the day as a whole.

Note Hierarchy

Good note takers can identify a hierarchy of ideas based on their note's overall structure and other clues, such as the style of font chosen for each piece of information and the use of dividers and containers. Sketchnoting reinforces this skill by forcing the note taker to think about the big ideas and ways to emphasize them. As a sketchnoter, you are often listening, analyzing, and figuring out what has the most meaning to you, and then creating meaning through your symbols and font choices. As you develop your skills, you will also start to notice patterns that develop based on how your brain is making those connections visually.

Because your eyes are drawn to visuals, you have to develop the skills to emphasize the right points. You also have the added benefit of making a more pleasing note to come back to and study later. As an English teacher, I expected my students to take notes, but I never directly taught the art of note taking until I started researching and practicing sketchnotes myself. I see now that I was missing an opportunity to help students make more meaning and connections with their learning, especially at the secondary level. Don't repeat my mistake. By teaching students to think about the structure of their notes, to use different fonts, colors, and containers to pull the eye to important points, you will explicitly teach students about note hierarchy.

Fonts

Your handwriting or font choice is one of the easiest ways to draw the eye to your note's most important points. As you see below, writing in all capital letters, going over your word a couple of times to create a bold effect, and changing the color all draw the eye. When I introduce font choice to students, I usually use the word "hello," because it's a simple to spell and allows them to practice font options. I typically tell students to identify three types of fonts for their sketchnotes:

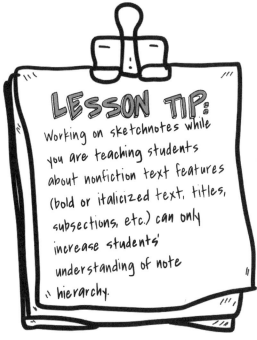

LESSON TIP:
Working on sketchnotes while you are teaching students about nonfiction text features (bold or italicized text, titles, subsections, etc.) can only increase students' understanding of note hierarchy.

- Regular handwriting, which is for most of the sketchnote's text

- A big and bold font for titles

- A font for special direct quotes, which can also be put in a container to show importance

Scan the QR code to watch a great video from Sketcho Frenzy about typography. This would be appropriate to show in classrooms.

Arrows

Arrows and similar connectors allow us to tie one idea to the next. It is incredibly important to do this physically on the paper to help trigger a connection in the brain too. Arrows can also draw the eye to important information. Depending on how you draw the arrows you could point out important information *and* connections.

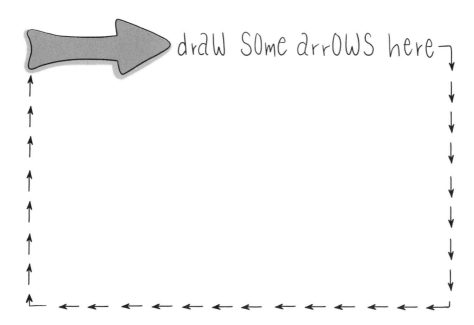

draw some arrows here

Dividers

You can use dividers to delineate a title or to indicate a vocabulary word and definition pair. I typically use a divider only when defining a new vocabulary word: The word goes on top of the divider with the definition on the bottom. There is no right or wrong way to use these elements, however; it, again, is personal preference.

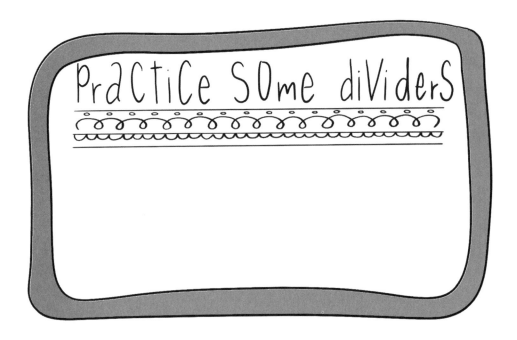

Containers & Banners

The last and final pieces for the basics of sketchnotes are containers and banners, which are similar but drawn slightly differently. Both are used to make up the structure of a modular sketchnote or added sporadically in any sketchnote to show hierarchy. For example, you can draw a container around an important quote, definition, thought, or question to catch the eye. Often you may write or draw something and then realize its importance later the more you listen or learn. To signify that importance, go back and put a container around it. Containers can be as simple as a circle, rectangle, speech bubble, or thought bubble. I like to jazz up the rectangles, though, to look like banners. Give it a try.

PraCtiCe COntainerS:

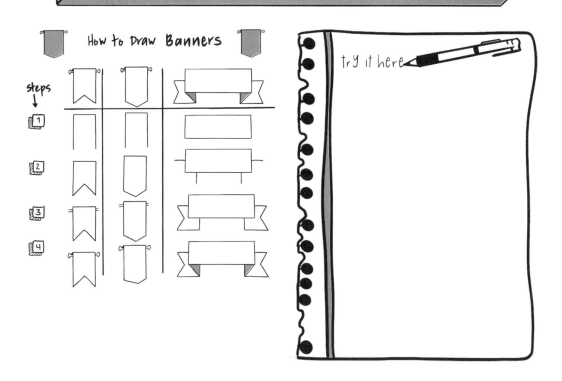

How to Draw Banners

steps

1

2

3

4

try it here

Advanced Technique: Headers

Another way to gather attention in your structure or note hierarchy, headers are a combination of containers, fonts, and dividers. You can use these for more detailed notes that will include multiple subjects or subheadings, such as when reading a textbook or working from a long lecture outline. Similar to containers or banners, headers combine a few techniques, which ultimately takes practice, on-the-spot thinking, or setup ahead of time.

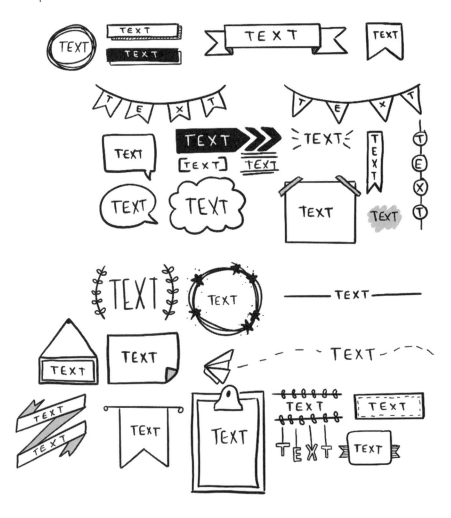

Implementation of Sketchnote Basics

To get access to the mini course on this chapter scan this QR code and enter the password.

My recommendation is to go through the sketchnoting basics with your students as an introductory lesson. You can use the previous sections as a guide for how to get students started drawing, and be sure to draw along with them. For more help, scan the QR code on this page to access a mini course on this chapter, as well as a one-page handout, which you can provide to secondary students to keep as a reference in their binders. Additionally, there is also a flipbook option, which can be printed, folded, and glued into readers' or writers' journals.

After your intro lesson, try using an article or a read-aloud to do some revisited sketchnotes as they are often more approachable than sketchnoting in real time (see Chapter 6 for more detail). In the next chapter, we will investigate some tools available for sketchnoting in the classroom.

CHAPTER 5

ANALOG VERSUS DIGITAL

In this chapter we will start looking at the tools used for sketchnoting, these can be either paper and pen (analog) or digital options like a tablet and a stylus. Having access to both is important to the learner. Letting students, as well as yourself, try the different modes is an important step towards identifying what feels more comfortable and natural for the sketchnoter. It can be a stumbling block in the process if you are using the wrong tools for your learning style. The analog versions can be simple: a piece of notebook paper and a pencil, or poster paper and pens of multiple colors and widths. The digital versions can range from a tablet with a free app, such as an iPad with Paper by WeTransfer, to a high-end iPad Pro and Apple Pencil.

Exploring Sketchnoting Styles

As you introduce sketchnotes, there is a benefit to first focusing on only the skills of sketchnoting. Specifically, I have found that teaching students how to use a new software program at the same time as teaching them the basics of sketchnotes can be incredibly difficult for them. It adds another layer of complexity that isn't always needed. I recommend doing intro lessons on sketchnoting separately from intro lessons on tools, such as apps or websites. That being said, it is important to note that there are differences between taking sketchnotes on paper and taking sketchnotes on a touchscreen device, as you'll learn in the upcoming sections. The ease of use for the learner must be taken into account, as well as ensuring the tools aren't getting in the way of the process.

In 2014, Pam Mueller and Daniel Oppenheimer published an article in *Psychological Science* that detailed their research about taking notes in class. They studied students who took notes with a computer and those that took notes via paper and pencil. Many non-digital natives reference this study as the ultimate argument for why technology should not be used in class. Those that take this approach are missing the whole point, however; the takeaway from this study is about the act of synthesizing the information heard in a lecture. You have to synthesize when you take paper and pencil notes, as well as sketchnotes, because it is harder to keep up with the content. Those students who were typing were not synthesizing; they were taking notes on everything. It is easier to take word-for-word notes when you are typing, because you can type faster than you can write. Faster, however, doesn't necessarily mean better for the learner. Ultimately, good note taking has to do with the synthesis and connections you make while you are learning. Students need to think about their learning and choose the most effective tools to enhance it, whether those are digital or analog, as well as the very style of note taking they are doing.

You want to give students confidence in the components of sketchnoting, as well as confidence in the tools they are using. Some people really gravitate towards art and stationery supplies. To them, like me, the idea of new pens, highlighters, and journals is as exciting as Christmas morning. Identify these students, and help guide them towards analog sketchnotes and developing their style: Ask them to pinpoint their favorite pen or highlighter for taking notes and why one pen feels better on a piece of paper than another.

On the other hand, some students gravitate towards learning the newest programs or devices and love the idea of quick edits and changes. I am one of these people also. Help guide students to identify their style, and give them the opportunity to discover which medium is right for them. Ironically, I have done enough introspection to be able to identify that I enjoy an analog journal and planner, but prefer to take sketchnotes digitally.

Analog Tools

For analog sketchnotes, students really don't need that many tools. Access to pencils, paper, and, at the very least, one extra color is enough to get started. While teaching sketchnotes, you are focusing on the hierarchy of notes, as I have mentioned before, and you want the students to think about color as a way to draw the eye to main ideas and other important information. Sometimes too many color choices in the moment can be distracting. Some of my favorite sketchnote artists only use two colors, black and one complimentary color. For instance, I typically use black and a blue color. However, sometimes when you are just learning your skills, adding color or labeling your drawing will help to remind you what your image actually is when you are revisiting your notes later.

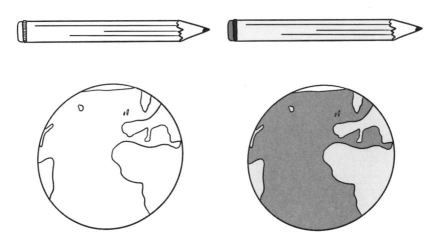

In terms of paper, it is best to encourage sketchnotes on every kind of paper, especially for those students that truly identify with sketchnotes. I find it hard to focus or process a meeting or information without sketching. Allowing students flexibility and freedom to doodle is key—whether in the margins of articles, their readers, their writer's notebooks, or elsewhere. I do think, however, that sometimes lines on a paper can be limiting in determining the direction of your sketchnotes. For example, I typically like to draw in landscape mode, but if I am given a piece of lined notebook paper, I feel almost forced to draw in portrait mode, because rotating it to landscape mode results in distracting vertical lines. Personally, I think it takes a lot of practice and knowledge about your preferences to see past the lines. So allowing access to printer paper at times would be helpful, as well. Access to printer paper at all times will help make that decision even easier.

The same techniques, tools, and skills that help students sketch their notes can help them with larger poster assignments, as well. Although the paper is larger, posters rely on all the same elements as sketchnotes to highlight important information, make connections, and engage the viewer. With their new visual vocabulary and understanding of the tools available, students can better show what they know.

Digital Tools

For digital tools, I definitely recommend a touchscreen device and a stylus. Regardless of what device you are using, you will also need an app or a web-based product. There isn't a specific app just for sketchnoting, because sketchnoting is simply a form of note taking that is personalized for the note taker. Instead, you can use a typical drawing app. For Android and iOS devices, I recommend Adobe Draw or WeTransfer's Paper; both are free. If you are using a touchscreen laptop device, you can try a web-based drawing or whiteboard program, such as AWW App or Sketch.io's Sketchpad.

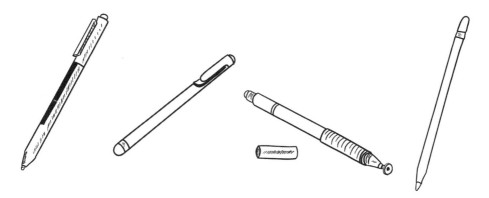

My preferred method of taking notes is with my iPad Pro (one of the big ones so I have lots room), an Apple Pencil, and the Procreate app. Procreate is not free, but is a great investment after you practice a bit and realize sketchnoting is something you want to take more seriously. Prior to having an Apple Pencil, I used a comparatively inexpensive Adonit Jot Pro stylus. I typically prefer a fine-tip stylus to one with a thicker rubber end, because I can more easily draw fine details. If you are outfitting an entire class with styli, the discount store inexpensive option works too!

Apps & Styli

The following list provides more information and links to help you get started in the world of digital note taking:

 PAPER (free, WeTransfer) is a free sketching app that has several drawing tools and an unlimited color palette. It is very intuitive and easy to get started with.
paper.bywetransfer.com

 ADOBE ILLUSTRATOR DRAW (free, Adobe) is a free drawing app that enables you to draw in layers to create more detailed and nuanced results.
www.adobe.com/products/draw.html

 DOODLE BUDDY (free, Doodle Buddy Labs) is a good option for little ones, allows students to draw with their fingers, and has an interface that is very easy to get started with.
www.doodlebuddy.co

PROCREATE (paid, Savage Software) is the most robust drawing app out there with a multitude of drawing tools, as well as the ability to pick up paint colors from any image. Plus, you can download tools from other users and even buy more options. You can find additional palettes of colors and different brushes on the Procreate site, as well as through third-party developers, some for purchase and some for free. For instance you could create your own unique brush and share it for other people to use. This is the app that most people use when they get serious about digital art. It is what I use.

procreate.art

SKETCHPAD (free, Sketch.io) is a browser-based drawing program. It's easy to search for on a touchscreen Chromebook, for example, and it offers plenty of options for tools and colors. Students do not have to create a profile to get started.

sketch.io/sketchpad

AWW APP (free, AWW) is a browser-based whiteboard drawing app. It is easy to use on a touchscreen device and even allows you to share a whiteboard with another user. To share whiteboards you have to create an account, but to draw with limited options you do not. It's easy to save a drawing to your drive, and AWW App has an infinite canvas as long as you use the zoom in and out feature.

Awwapp.com

ZITEBOARD (free; Ziteboard) is another browser-based whiteboard drawing app that is easy to get started with. It also has similar infinite canvas and sharing capabilities as Aww app. Let students try a few of these and decide on their own which is their favorite.

www.ziteboard.com

ADONIT PRO is my second-favorite stylus after the Apple Pencil. If you do not have a device that supports the Apple Pencil, the Adonit Pro is the one to get. It has a fine tip that makes creating detail easy.

www.adonit.net/jot/pro

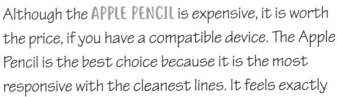

Although the APPLE PENCIL is expensive, it is worth the price, if you have a compatible device. The Apple Pencil is the best choice because it is the most responsive with the cleanest lines. It feels exactly like you are writing with a pencil to paper.

www.apple.com/apple-pencil

Digital Resources

Once you have your new tools, here are two useful resources to help you practice sketchnoting:

 SKETCHNOTES WITH NICHOLE: Follow along with me in some drawing tutorials on YouTube. I go over all the basics from Chapter 4!
youtu.be/ppYXHOnhquc

 SKILLSHARE COURSE ON PROCREATE: Skillshare is a site where people create online classes for creative projects and arts—including Procreate. You can also find additional classes on other apps and types of illustrating. Accounts are free, but you can access more features if you upgrade to a paid Premium account. I love my account and take classes in illustration and visuals, and more.
skl.sh/2B30bBw

Analog versus Digital Quiz

Still don't know where you fall? Take the following quiz to find out.

Circle Yes or No. Go with your gut, and don't overthink it.

1. Do you own a pencil case?	Yes	No
2. Do you have access to a touchscreen device?	Yes	No
3. Do you own highlighters?	Yes	No
4. Do you have a nice stylus?	Yes	No
5. Can you get a highlighter in your hand in less than 5 minutes?	Yes	No
6. Do you learn new apps or websites quickly?	Yes	No
7. Do you still organize your papers in binders or folders?	Yes	No
8. Do you watch tutorials on Youtube when you get stuck?	Yes	No
9. Do you buy notebooks or journals?	Yes	No
10. Have you seen sketchnotes online, and can you identify which are digital and which are analog?	Yes	No
11. Do you buy or use sticky notes?	Yes	No
12. Do you like the look of digital notes better than analog?	Yes	No
13. Do you have a favorite pen or pencil?	Yes	No
14. Do you keep up to date with tech gadget trends?	Yes	No
15. Do you own so many pens that friends have pointed it out?	Yes	No
16. Do you follow digital illustration or artists on social media?	Yes	No
17. Do you own a ruler?	Yes	No
18. Do you like to draw or write in pencil because you make a lot of mistakes?	Yes	No
19. Do you know what washi tape is?	Yes	No
20. Do you like to have access to a lot of tools and color choices without having to carry around a ton of supplies?	Yes	No

If you circled yes for more odd numbered questions, you should try your hand at analog sketchnotes. If you circled yes for more even numbered questions, you're in the digital sketchnote camp. If you are evenly split, try both and figure out which works best for your needs.

CHAPTER 6

REAL-TIME VERSUS REVISITED STRATEGIES

After getting students used to the different components of sketchnoting and letting them wrap their minds around this way of taking notes, it is time to start introducing different styles of note taking. For example, for real-time sketchnotes you draw live while you are listening to a lecture or watching a video. Alternately, revisited sketchnotes can be used when note taking is less time sensitive. With this approach, you revisit content that has possibly already been consumed in another way, such as close reading of an article or watching a video and taking quick bulleted notes. Revisited sketchnotes are easier to approach when you are first learning because of that lack of time sensitivity. Real-time sketchnotes challenge your listening comprehension skills and can be applied in a variety of situations from lectures, to meetings, to videos and podcasts.

Real-Time Sketchnotes

Practicing Listening Skills
Information is Coming Fast
Structure is Important
Simple Art vs. Fancy Art

Revisited Sketchnotes

Information Has Already Been Consumed
Take Your Time
Revisit Content
Ability to Be More Specific
With Structure & Art

Which Version Should You Start with in Class?

When you start working with students on sketchnotes, you'll notice that the act of drawing even single-word symbols takes a lot of skill and practice to the uninitiated. Think about the Graphic Jam activity in Chapter 1. Drawing an item in 10 seconds can be difficult, and it usually is for students new to sketchnoting. Now imagine trying to draw while also trying to comprehend a lecture's content. The average lecturer, video, or podcast is going to go much, much faster than short staccato bursts of one word every 10 seconds. Sketchnoting in real time can be like trying to juggle with mittens on. For this reason alone, I recommend doing revisited sketchnotes as your introduction to sketchnotes.

For example, in a revisited sketchnote session, the information has already been consumed, you aren't learning anything new so you can take your time. This could take the form of reading an article and practicing close reading strategies, as well as highlighting and annotating the key points. Next, turn those highlights and annotations into a sketchnote. You could also have students jot down information on a KWL (know, want to know, learned) chart or take quick bullet-point notes while watching a video, then give them time to revisit those in-the-moment notes and generate a sketchnote from that content to show comprehension and connections that can't be seen in the original form of notes—thus revisiting the content. You can also combine the revisited approach with taking another form of notes, such as Cornell Notes, and either create a sketchnote of that information or add a layer of doodles, containers, arrows, and so on to the preexisting Cornell notes.

Often students are more used to annotating or highlighting important key phrases in a text, because this is something that teachers will take the time to model for them. These are note taking skills traditionally taught in the classroom. In fact, sketchnotes could become a great way to make revisiting notes and content relevant where it might not have been before. After the students take those more traditional close reading notes, have them take that next step to show connections and comprehension by using sketchnotes. When they are given this revisiting time, students have the ability to take their time and be specific about their form or layout, and they can take more time to make those all important connections. You as the teacher can even prompt those connections while they are working on their sketchnotes.

Revisiting content, such as a highlighted article or a previously read chapter, allows students to better summarize the content and get out of the habit of writing down all the content verbatim. The act of synthesizing in sketchnotes is one of its biggest attributes in aiding retention of content.

Listening Comprehension Strategies

Besides realizing through sketchnotes that I previously did my students a great disservice by teaching just the general basics on note taking, I also realized that there was a whole genre of listening comprehension that I didn't even touch on. What do we as learners need to focus on? Once students are more comfortable with their visual vocabulary, sketchnoting can help boost their listening comprehension skills as well. Learners need to focus on what Dan Roam calls "verbal-visual 'trigger' phrases" in his book *Blah Blah Blah: What to*

Do When Words Don't Work. Learners need to listen for the who, what, how much, where, when, how, and why of the subject being discussed. These are a learner's essential cognitive questions and filtering tools. With these in mind, students have to start putting the key facts and important details into their sketchnotes by thinking about:

- How do my ideas on the information take form?

- How much of what I am learning do I have to show?

- What connections can I make to what I have already learned?

- How does this learning work moving forward, and why does it matter to me?

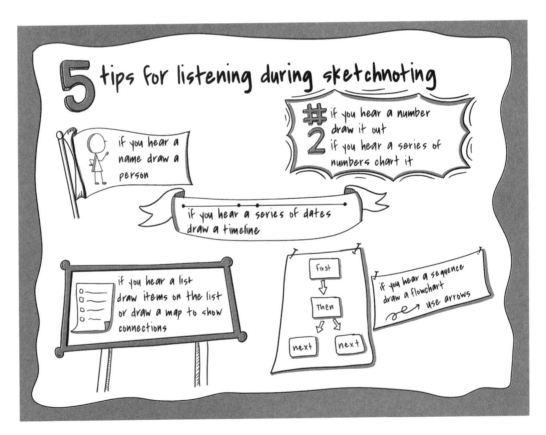

When students are actively listening they should be able to hear a thought, process it, synthesize it, and then make connections to that content. Students will need to practice the skill of active listening: being able to retain the information that is important and dump what isn't. They need to sketchnote the important information, which sometimes needs to be placed in short-term memory while they are continuing to sketchnote. In the best notes, students elaborate with prior content knowledge and make connections. Flexible interpretation is also important; remember, your interpretation of the content is going to produce a different outcome than another listener's. If the note makes sense to you, that is the most important part.

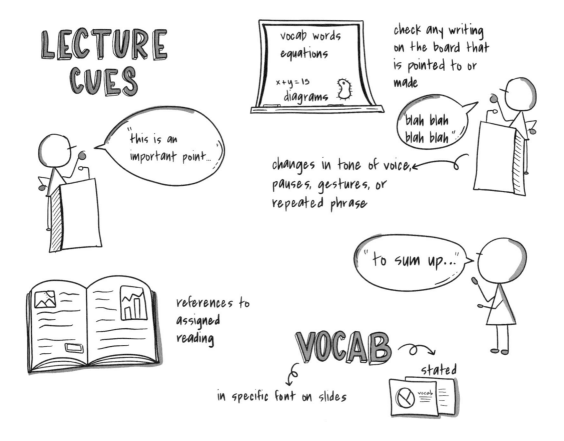

Again, the practice of listening comprehension is extremely important; over time students will build stamina, which is the culmination of mastering all the skills needed for real-time sketchnotes. Eventually, you and your students may even find it hard to sit in a class, lecture, or meeting and not take sketchnotes, because it has become a part of your natural processing.

Strategies to Build Speed During Real-Time Sketchnotes

For you and students to build up speed you must practice as much as you can. You can find plenty of resources online to help: sketchnoting challenges to participate in, hashtags to follow, and doodle tutorial videos to watch (see Chapter 13 for specific suggestions).

The more you build up your visual vocabulary, the easier it is to draw whatever you are thinking quickly. If you are about to introduce a topic to your students, think about what they might need to be able to draw to be successful. If you are reading a story with a character in a wheelchair, how might they draw that? If your class is going to be learning about electricity, how could they draw that? Doing quick online searches or working with your students ahead of time to come up with symbols will ultimately make the in-the-moment drawings come easier.

Some podcasts will allow you to slow down the audio, YouTube allows you to speed up or slow down the video as well. If you find that sketchnoting in real-time is too fast for your students, therefore, you can slow down and gradually come back to real-time speed as students start to build up their skills.

7 Tips For Improving Real-Time Sketchnotes

Practice Making Connections with arrows

Practice being able to focus on what you are listening to.

Get your title and speaker down beforehand.

You should be critically thinking about what is the most important content and should be included. To practice this, try watching a TED talk. After you watch it once, watch it one more time to see if you missed anything. Do this with a partner as well, see what they catch that you miss

Review the topic or material to make sure you know how to draw the items that might come up.

Identify the goals or objectives for the lesson or lecture. If someone says

Three important things

Write down numbers 1, 2, 3 and be on the listening lookout for those three items.

Identify your three main fonts!

fonts

▪Title

▪All main writing

▪Important Quotes

Another trick is to listen at normal speed and if at the time you are running out of ideas on how to draw something or map something out, take good old-fashioned notes on a post-it if you are taking analog sketchnotes. Or in a digital platform, you can easily add another layer or write out the traditional notes, then erase them once you draw out your ideas related to them. This is a different approach for revisited sketchnotes. I have known some educators that take normal bulleted notes during the original lecture or conference session and revisit those notes after the session to make their sketchnotes.

The Four Cs of 21st Century Learning

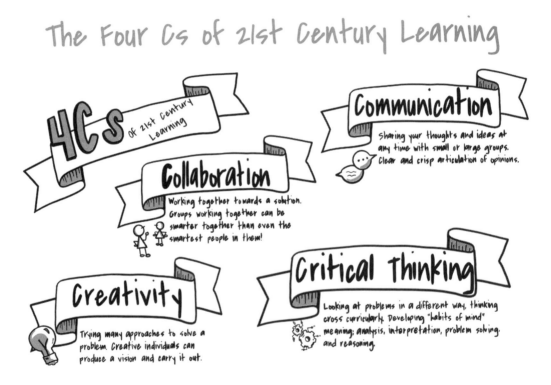

4Cs Of 21st Century Learning

Communication
Sharing your thoughts and ideas at any time with small or large groups. Clear and crisp articulation of opinions.

Collaboration
Working together towards a solution. Groups working together can be smarter together than even the smartest people in them!

Creativity
Trying many approaches to solve a problem. Creative individuals can produce a vision and carry it out.

Critical Thinking
Looking at problems in a different way, thinking cross curricularly. Developing "habits of mind" meaning; analysis, interpretation, problem solving, and reasoning.

Teachers need to be able to complement traditional content knowledge with work in the Four Cs of 21st Century Learning to prepare students for today's global workforce. Sketchnoting fits right in with all of the Four Cs. Sketchnotes are a way for students to visualize their learning and communicate their ideas in a new and creative way. Students can easily highlight their questions, ideas, and solutions. They also are actively working on critical thinking by synthesizing information and reaching for links to prior knowledge and across different disciplines. Obviously, they are also tapping into creativity in trying to approach note taking in a new way. For more information on the Four Cs, scan the QR code for a great report from the NEA, which helped guide some lesson ideas in later chapters.

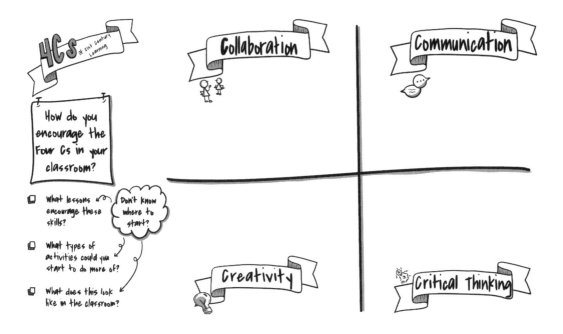

The only one that is a bit of a stretch is collaboration; however, I have found that when you are working on a sketchnote, taking the time to turn to an elbow partner to see what their sketchnote has that yours might be lacking is a way to add more depth to your sketchnote. This is an especially important skill for students while doing live sketchnotes and practicing their listening comprehension. Group poster making and collaborative sketchnotes obviously would require working with a group.

"The future belongs to a very different kind of person with a very different kind of mind- creators and empathizers, pattern recognizers and meaning makers. These people... will now reap society's richest rewards and share its greatest joys."
A Whole New Mind: Why Right-Brainers Will Rule the Future By Daniel H. Pink

Today's students need to be able to make connections, and think critically to someday solve global issues. Are we giving them enough opportunities to do that? With the increase of connectivity, students may be called upon to work in global teams and have a basic understanding of cultural competencies and the ability to communicate with a wide variety of people. Let's try an activity. Scan the QR codes on the following pages and practice some sketchnote skills, keeping in mind the Four Cs of 21st Century Learning.

HOW WOULD YOU CHANGE THE WORLD?

What would you change about the world? Sketchnote ideas that come to you as you watch the video. Work into the sketchnote an explanation of what you would change about the world, and include examples.

Video: How Would You Change the World? | 0-100

REAL-TIME VERSUS REVISITED STRATEGIES

HOW TO CHANGE THE WORLD

Sketchnote ideas that come to you as you watch the video, and work into your sketchnote your plan of action. If you could do just one thing this year to make a difference, what will it be?

Video: How To Change The World (A Work In Progress)

SECTION II

SKETCHNOTES ACROSS CONTENT AREAS

CHAPTER 7   Sketchnotes in Science Class

CHAPTER 8   Sketchnotes in Social Studies

CHAPTER 9   Sketchnotes in ELA

CHAPTER 10   Sketchnotes in Math

CHAPTER 11   Assessment & Evaluation

CHAPTER 7

SKETCHNOTES IN SCIENCE CLASS

Science can often be heavy with new vocabulary terms and complex concepts, which means specialized drawings will be needed for sketchnotes. To make sure that students can be successful when they are going through dense information, model with them and think ahead to assist with any science-type doodles that could stop their note-taking synthesis. The symbols and images should come easily and not get in the way of students learning and making connections. Making sure that students are aware of upcoming abbreviations and equations, as well as how they might represent those in their notes, is also key.

Remind students to cross-reference their sketchnotes with previous lab notes or reading notes. If they are taking sketchnotes with a lecture, remind students to get out their corresponding lab notes or reading notes, and vice versa. To me, the diagrams that are associated with science lessons lead to a natural progression into sketchnotes. Beyond those diagrams, however, let's look at a few other ways you could use sketchnotes in the classroom.

Lab Write-ups

Giving students the freedom to sketchnote their lab write-ups, or allowing them to use some of the principles of sketchnotes in the lab write-up, will help shape some of the lab's expectations, as well as force students to make connections that they might not have made without the added time and framework. The sample lesson plan that follows illustrates how to integrate sketchnotes into the process.

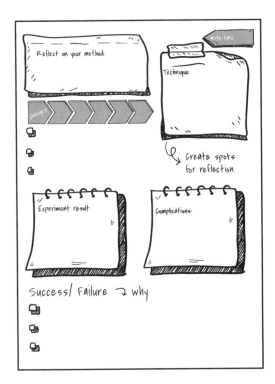

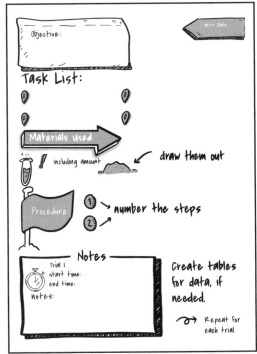

Summary

GRADE LEVEL: 6-12

OBJECTIVE: Getting students to take more thorough notes during a lab by reflecting and making connections through their sketchnotes.

TIME ALLOTMENT: 20 extra minutes on a lab.

Give students time before they start their lab experiment to create some of the necessary components in their notes.

Give them time after the lab to write their results, complications, and reasons for success or failure.

Implementation

1. OPENER:

   Talk to students about your expectations for lab notes.

   a. Labs can take several days so date your pages; this is important.

   b. Make an objective "I will…" statement to help frame the experiment.

   c. List out your tasks: What is it that you have to complete in all of your trials?

   d. Record all the materials that you use. Make sure to list the amount used and brand (if that is important), and then draw each item if at all possible.

   e. Sequentially list your procedure. This is different from your tasks; the procedure is a list of actions.

   f. Create tables and fill-in-the-blank forms so you can focus on the experiment, rather than randomly writing down pieces that don't matter to the ultimate result.

   g. Make notes wherever something unexpected happens.

   h. Reflect on your method and technique steps, even if you are following them from a textbook.

   i. Note any complications or concerns during your experiment.

   j. Describe your expected results versus your actual results and whether you think your experiment was successful or not.

2. DIRECT INSTRUCTION:

   a. Model an example sketchnote for the lab you are about to begin with the students.

   b. Perhaps even showcase how you would draw any of the materials or how you would show the formula or expected changes or outcomes of the experiment. (This is something you will need to do less and less as students become more familiar with lab notes.)

3. INDEPENDENT WORK:

   Proceed with the lab as usual, prompting students with how to draw certain elements as they might come to each in their experiment.

   For example, if something is supposed to reach a certain temperature, show them how they might illustrate that.

FOLLOW-UP ACTIVITIES

You could have students come back to their notes to revisit and show correlations between one lab and the next. You could even have students sketchnote the correlation from two labs on a new spread in their lab notebooks.

TIPS & TRICKS

There are plenty of doodles out there for science and lab items. To see a science doodle playlist and find additional tools for your students, scan the QR code.

Lab Rules

Often at the start of the year or at the beginning of the year's very first lab, science teachers go through safety procedures for their lab and even present a safety contract. What better way to get the students to show what they know about being safe in the lab than to have them create a sketchnote demonstrating those safety rules? You can choose to do this a couple of ways. For example, you could have students create a poster for all rules, or you could jigsaw the rules and assign one rule per student so they each are clearly defining one rule. They should make a point to state the rule, what would happen if the rule is not followed, and how they could handle an accident if it should happen.

Summary

GRADE LEVEL: 6-12

OBJECTIVE: Students will learn why it is important to follow lab safety rules and will create their own safety rule sketchnote.

TIME ALLOTMENT: One class period to talk about lab safety, possibly run a model experiment for students outlining the safety rules. Either assign the sketchnote as homework or allow another class period or 60 minutes to create the sketchnote.

End-of-unit Review

Similar to an end-of-unit poster, have students do a sketchnote of important terms and definitions, as well as diagrams. If you have given adequate instruction and practice time on some of the components of sketchnoting, you should see logical connections formed, use of containers and arrows, and definitions called out in an eye-catching way.

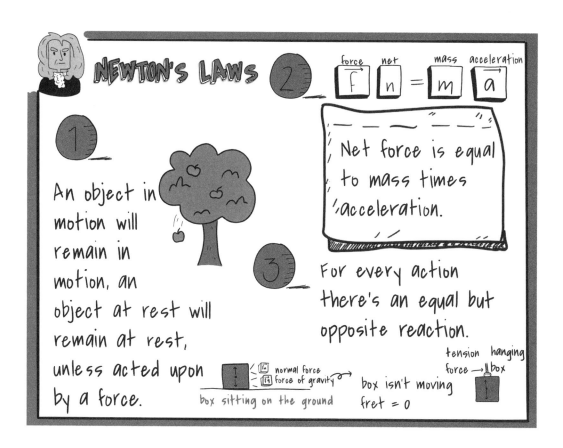

Summary

GRADE LEVEL: 4-12

OBJECTIVE: Students create an end-of-unit sketchnote, showcasing important terms and diagrams, using sketchnote techniques to draw the eye to the most important items and how items connect or relate.

TIME ALLOTMENT: One class period.

CLASSROOM VOICES

LEAH LACROSSE

8TH-GRADE SCIENCE TEACHER, OHIO
@llacrosse (Twitter), @lacrossescience (Instagram)

Sketchnoting in the science classroom has been an amazing process and tool for students to show their thinking, understanding, creativity, and further questions with the content. Using this process with students allows me to connect with various learners in ways that haven't always been possible.

I've found that modeling sketchnoting with students is an important step that shouldn't be skipped. Showing students how to organize, build, and connect ideas is a process that should be scaffolded. Doing this early and often helps build student confidence, skill, and depth in sketchnoting.

The biggest challenge at first in using sketchnoting in the classroom is to help build up student confidence. The initial reaction is doubt in their artistic and technical skills. Once we work through the various ways to show content and thinking, students move away from critiquing their artistic skills and begin to develop their own style and organization.

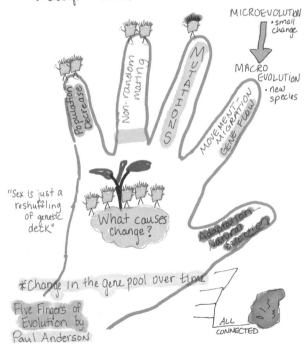

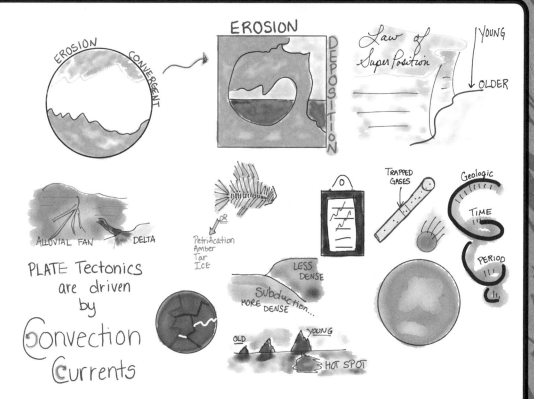

EROSION

DEPOSITION

CONVERGENT

EROSION

Law of Super Position

YOUNG

OLDER

TRAPPED GASES

Geologic

TIME

PERIOD

ALLUVIAL FAN   DELTA

Petrification
Amber
Tar
Ice

OR

LESS DENSE

Subduction...

MORE DENSE

OLD   YOUNG

HOT SPOT

PLATE Tectonics
are driven
by
Convection
Currents

One favorite way that I use sketchnoting with students early on is with short TED and TED-ED videos. The content is very well organized and usually has some visual prompts that are helpful for students. As a great starting activity, I choose a video that is about 5 to 10 minutes long, and I build the lesson in stages. The first view of the video, we simply watch the video and have a discussion about information that is new, known, and interesting. In the second view of the video, I ask students to start by setting up their sketchnote on an iPad in the Paper (WeTransfer) app with their name, the date, and the video title. We watch the video again and find three to five words or concepts that are central to the video. As the video ends, I switch the view over to my iPad; students share their words with me and watch how I utilize the software. I highlight how to

build a concept map with the words while demonstrating how to use connecting arrows, symbols, and organization. In the third viewing of the video, I mute the audio and ask students to just watch the video. They are instructed to find three to five images that can be thought of as central to the video. As they select them, they begin to flesh out their sketchnote with these images. Time is given after the movie to chat with each other while finalizing these drawings. While they are drawing and elaborating their sketchnotes, my iPad is mirrored to the projector to show more tips and tricks with the app, as well as how I weave the images into the words. I dedicate the time to these early activities so that students get the practice with the software while learning the science content as they build.

CHAPTER 8

SKETCHNOTES IN SOCIAL STUDIES

Students can often feel overwhelmed by dates, new concepts, and new vocabulary in social studies. They then struggle to absorb all of the information they need to be able to create notes in manageable sections or chunks. Whether they are reading a textbook chapter or listening to a lecture, the act of *pre-reading* is especially helpful. For example, previewing a chapter, taking a look at the subtitles, or even reading the first sentence of each paragraph can help get students' minds ready for the key topics and vocabulary. Likewise, if students are about to listen to a lecture, getting a sense of the lecture's theme ahead of time will help them key into what to listen for.

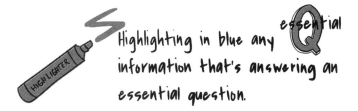

Highlighting in blue any essential information that's answering an essential question.

Highlighting in green any information that applies to a specific course framework.

Highlighting in yellow any vocab words especially those that are bolded in the textbook.

You can set students up for success by reminding them to pre-read a chapter, article, or short YouTube video on the topic to get their brains ready. Or even provide a brief summary of key concepts, vocabulary, and people on the projector as students walk in. If students know how to re-create these items or people in icons or drawings, sketchnoting will go more smoothly. Additionally, students could plan to highlight specific types of information with unique colors to further prioritize information. Finally, flowcharts and timelines can be used to great effect when enhanced by the sketchnote principles.

Current Events

When students read newspapers or magazines (in print or online) or watch videos of current events, they become more familiar with informational writing and more critical readers of the news. We want students to gain knowledge of the world around them in local, national, and international communities. Allowing them to sketchnote their understanding of current events enables students to make deeper connections to those events and to what they are learning. To help students, model this skill of seeking out connections by creating your own sketchnotes of current events, showing the deeper connections that you have due to your expertise on the subject. Sketchnotes help with retention, which in turn improves students' understanding when they have discussions with classmates or family. The sample lesson plan that follows offers ideas on how to get started with current event sketchnotes and possible presentations.

Title: "Slime Eels Release mucus on Oregon Highway"

Author: Jason Bittel

Who: A truck on a highway crashed

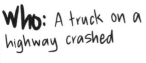

When: July 2017

Vocab:

Hagfish: deep-sea scavengers

Viscoelastic filament microfibers that form a semi-solid gel.

What: Eels let out mucus when stressed.

Slime

Why: Hagfish fisheries supply the fish to Asian markets - prized dish.

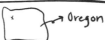

Where: Oregon Highway

Oregon

Free Drawing space/ summary/ connections

Slime is defensive

Hagfish (deep sea)

Bulldozer to clean slime

many eels died in crash

Summary

GRADE LEVEL: 3-12

OBJECTIVE: For students to read and understand informational text, as well as gain knowledge of current events. Through sketchnotes, students practice their synthesis and connections between current events and what they already know from past events. If students share their sketchnotes and what they learned from the current event, they will additionally work on speaking skills.

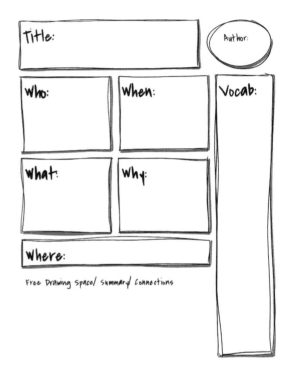

TIME ALLOTMENT: 45 minutes to read and create their sketchnotes. If you are having students share out, allow 5-10 minutes per student.

Implementation

1. **OPENER:**

   a. Tell students you will be regularly looking at current event articles and doing a sketchnote and presentation on those current events.

    b. Tell students to use their typical close-reading and annotation techniques when reading an article. They should focus on making sure they can answer the Five Ws: who, what, when, where, and why.

    c. Giving them a Sketchnote template could also be helpful. Scan the QR code to get access to ten template options.

2. DIRECT INSTRUCTION:

    a. Tell students to read the article and annotate.

    b. As the students finish their first pass of the article, have them go back and begin their sketchnote by chunking the text by paragraphs. They should be able to summarize each paragraph with words or symbols. If there is a word that sticks out, such as a vocabulary word, tell students they should draw it in a way that catches the eye. If there is a specific place listed, tell them to map it. Again, they should be able to draw or write about each of the Five Ws. Model this a few times with students, doing a whole class example at least once.

3. INDEPENDENT WORK:

    a. Give students time to locate information in the article.

    b. Using a graphic organizer for the first couple of times might help students that struggle with answering the questions of who, what, when, where, and why in their sketchnotes.

    c. Allow students time to draw their understanding of the current event.

FOLLOW-UP ACTIVITIES

If you are going to have students present their current event sketchnotes, give them time to prepare. Each should tell the class their article's title and make sure to point out the main points of the article.

Additionally, they can answer questions like:

- Why was this a significant event?
- What effect does this have on our community?
- What is your opinion on this event?
- Is there a problem posed in this event, and does it have a solution?

TIPS & TRICKS

- You could work on a group sketchnote on a piece of poster paper: Have students work together on an article and then share out in a group. This would reduce share-out time, if the speaking component was an issue due to lack of time.
- Have students sign up on a calendar so they know when they are sharing their current event sketchnote and can be prepared.
- Use sites like Newsela.com for article curation and assignment to make selecting age- and level-appropriate texts easy for you and your students.
- For the Who category, have students try to draw a person or thing to symbolize.

Timelines

Encourage students to get creative with dates and events in a timeline by adding the basic components of sketchnoting. The end result will be more pleasing and memorable. To guide students, use an organizer that lists the dates and maybe the title of the events. Students can then write down more information and create their picture or symbol in the spaces provided.

Name _____ Date _____ Per _____

Sketchnote Timeline

Directions: Fill in the blank space for more information on each event, and then create a picture or symbol for each event in the square on the side. Draw your completed timeline with all information on the back.

Picture or Symbol

	Event Title / Date
	_____
	_____
	_____

	Event Title / Date
	_____
	_____
	_____

	Event Title / Date
	_____
	_____
	_____

	Event Title / Date
	_____
	_____
	_____

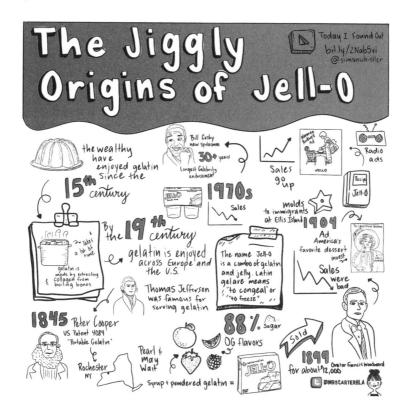

To wrap up the activity, have students flip their organizers over to draw a sketchnote that connects all the collected information. Additionally, remind students to use color, varied handwriting, arrows, connectors, dividers, containers, and bullets where necessary to help draw the eye to important information in the timeline.

In the sketchnote on the previous page, you can see the history, or origins of Jell-O. This came from watching a video on YouTube called, *The Jiggly Origins of Jell-O*. Scan the QR code, and try your hand at creating a timeline or sketchnote on the origins of Jell-O.

Scan here for The Jiggly Origins of Jell-O video from Today I Found Out.

Sketch here

Cause & Effect

When students study the cause and effect of an event in history, allow the principles of sketchnotes to jazz up the old Venn diagram graphic organizer, or allow students to sketchnote a flowchart to showcase their knowledge. Adding people and images can place emphasis on things you may or may not have listed and make graphic organizers more visually appealing, while allowing for greater recall.

Scan the QR cocde to watch a video from Sketcho Frenzy specifically about Venn diagrams.

Sketchnotes During Speeches

Having students sketchnote during their peers' presentations enables your class to work on speaking standards while also practicing their real-time sketchnote skills and listening

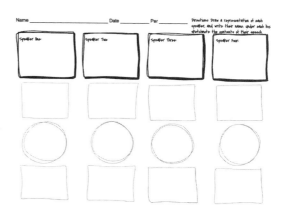

comprehension. Often real-time sketchnoting is difficult, as the act of synthesizing from just listening comprehension is a much more taxing skill. Depending on the length of the speeches, consider giving students an organizer to help them prioritize and present the content.

In the space provided, think about a few ways you could make listening to speakers easier for your students: What key features should they be listening for? How can you help them make connections? How can you fit information from multiple speakers on one sheet?

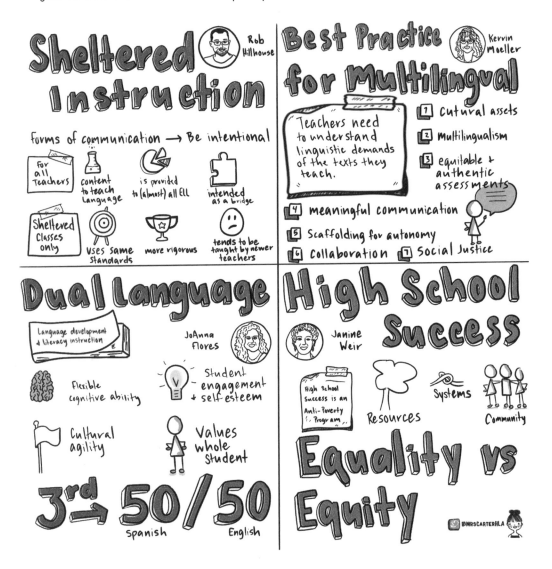

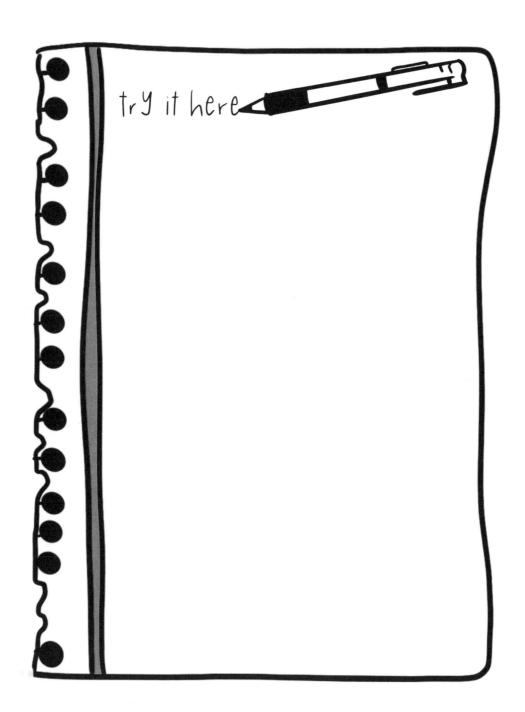

try it here

BETTINA CURL

5TH-GRADE TEACHER, OREGON
@BettinaCurl (Twitter), @Mrs.b_curl (Instagram)

Sketchnoting allows students at various learning levels multiple entry points to the curriculum and targets. Students are able to make connections to the content and apply new ways to synthesize their thoughts. I have found using sketchnoting for social studies supports my fifth-grade students to make better connections to the content. After introducing sketchnoting, I saw positive emotional effects for my special education students, as well as improvement in their ability to retain information. Students were able to engage multiple modalities in learning with sketchnoting, and it has provided a preemptive measure to stop students from losing focus in the acquisition of information.

Sketchnoting has been a huge support for many students, but some struggled to conceptualize their learning and thoughts during their first attempts. Not all students thought of themselves as artists, and it was hard for them to separate sketchnoting from art. This lack of confidence in their art can deter students from trying and being able to use the skill to support their learning. After students had a couple weeks of practice with the application of sketchnoting skills and strategies, however, they were more engaged, excited, and eager to learn.

When working with fifth graders, and elementary students in general, I find it important to create a visual vocabulary guide

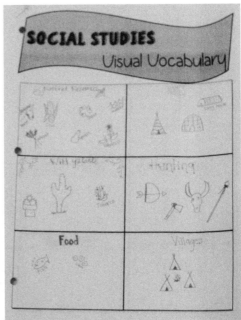

or dictionary to help students build a frame of reference in the beginning. I have a very diverse group of students and found that many of them pulled from their cultures' print or traditional art styles when creating their visual vocabulary lists.

When starting, we worked on many timed drills to develop fluency and confidence. It took a couple of weeks to develop the sketchnote mentality when note taking in class. Students would share details from their weekend or movies they saw, or I would give book talks while students practiced. (That's my favorite way to practice!) I would sometimes read the first page, read the blurb on the back cover, or share a book trailer.

Once the class was confident sketchnoting, we incorporated it into our social studies focus unit on native tribes and explorers. Students spent weeks researching Native tribes (Aztec,

Inca, Algonquin, Inuit, Pueblo, and Iroquois). Students were placed into tribe circles with one representative from each tribe. Using text and digital resources, students collected information about geography, homes, culture, food, natural resources, travel, and lifestyle.

Students independently gathered notes and created profiles for their tribes creating a visual presentation (the codex and digital). While collecting information, they created a visual vocabulary dictionary for themselves as a quick reference guide. They later used these dictionaries to assist them while taking notes during presentations or class lessons.

Students then returned to their tribe circles to present about their tribes. Representatives from other tribes recorded information to "return back to their tribes," and students took sketchnotes of each presentation.

CHAPTER 9

SKETCHNOTES IN ELA

We know that note taking as a standard is introduced in third grade, but students need consistent practice through the years and reinforcement across all the content areas. Ultimately what good note takers do is understand the difference between ideas and main ideas, details and key details. Good note takers can determine the importance of ideas and reflect that hierarchy in their notes, which in turn enhances their recall and comprehension when studying.

Even though I love highlighters, just highlighting something isn't the best way to study, take notes, or retain information. Using that highlighter or rendering important information with color in your sketchnotes as a part of a bigger note-taking strategy, however, is much more effective. Teachers need to model close reading strategies, help students identify how to highlight the essential details, and zero in on the specific information that the author wants readers to know. Text complexity increases as students get older, and not all the details in a book are the key details. Authors, like speakers, can shift in thought and go on a tangent before coming back to their main point. Good sketchnoters need to be able to identify those main points, whether they are reading text and converting to a sketch, or listening and real-time sketchnoting. This chapter offers ideas on how you can use sketchnotes in the English classroom and support students in becoming better note takers while reading, listening to lectures, and more.

Sketchnote a Plotline of a Story

Giving students the option to visualize the key features of a story's plotline will give them a better understanding of how to determine the importance of the story structure, as well as help them to retain the main ideas of the story. Students often need a lot of practice at seeing the patterns that are used to create a short story or novel. The lesson plan that follows should give students another tool in their toolbox for identifying this important literary element.

The Giver by Lois Lowry

Jonas leaves the community with Gabe.

Climax

Jonas understands that "release" means they are killed. He realizes Gabe will be released.

Jonas gets memory of war and pain. He is told about Rosemary the Giver's daughter.

They are pursued.

Falling Action

He gets the memory of color.

He gets the sled memory.

Jonas gets memories from The Giver.

Jonas receives his job as receiver of memories.

Rising Action

Jonas finds elsewhere.

Resolution

Exposition

Introduction to a "utopian" society where they have precision of language, no emotions, people who are too old or sick are "released." Jonas's family is taking care of an extra baby who is falling behind in his development.

Summary

GRADE LEVEL: 3-12

OBJECTIVE: Students will review the literary element of plot and demonstrate an understanding of plot structure by sketchnoting a plotline with a current text. The sketchnote should show their analysis of the plot of their current text.

TIME ALLOTMENT:

1. Session One: 20 minutes to go over plot structure in a mini-lesson

2. Session Two: 15 minutes to give students time to figure out the plotline points of their current text

3. Session Three: 30 minutes for students to draw their sketchnote of the plotline

Implementation

1. OPENER

    a. Explain that plot is a series of events that make up the story and that it can be seen in more than just novels read in class. It can be seen in TV, movies, and so on.

    b. Go over the main points of plot (exposition, rising action, climax, falling action, and resolution).

    c. Watch a short video. (Scan the QR Code on this page for a playlist of short storytelling videos.)

d. Model a class example of a sketchnote for one of these short video stories. Once you have shown an example, let students attempt it on one of their stories.

2. DIRECT INSTRUCTION

a. Have students explore some questions, such as:

   i. What does the author have to explain at the beginning for us to understand what is happening? (This is for the exposition.)

   ii. What event starts the rising action? How do we know the problem is being introduced?

   iii. When does the story peak? (This is for the climax.)

   iv. What events are leading to the problem being resolved? (This is for the falling action.)

   v. How is the problem, or the story, resolved? (This is for the resolution.)

b. When students have these ideas locked in, have them begin to sketchnote their plotline.

3. INDEPENDENT WORK

a. Allow students time to gather the information to create their sketchnote of the plotline.

b. Allow students time to create their sketchnote once they have analyzed their story.

FOLLOW-UP ACTIVITIES

- Have students attempt a plotline on different styles of stories: a short story, poem, narrative podcast, TV show, or movie.
- Have students think about or try to see patterns in different genres, such as mystery versus comedy, science fiction versus realistic fiction, or historical fiction versus biography.

TIPS & TRICKS

- Modeling a plotline several times with short stories or short video clips will help solidify the process for students to sketchnote a plotline on their own.
- If students are having a hard time with a section of the plotline, try asking questions about the other elements of the story. Ask students about issues between characters, ask about the setting, and so on.

Readers & Writers Workshop (Mini-Lessons)

The workshop model provides time for mini-lessons and one-on-one conferring. When you as a teacher use visuals during this time, the effect is the same as when the note taker does sketchnotes: Students can retain the information easier, and everyone involved benefits. Sketchnotes for mini-lessons should be clear and concise, and include a lot of icons. Depending on the students involved,

I recommend working together to create a sketchnote in their reader's or writer's notebooks on the content of the current mini-lesson. Eventually, when students start to better understand how to translate their mini-lesson into a sketchnote, you can allow the students to create on their own. If a student is still struggling, then working together provides another opportunity for them to explain what they interpreted from the mini-lesson itself. Every mini-lesson is a chance for students to create a sketchnote that pertains to them and their current writing or reading. For a ton of great ideas on mini-lessons, take a look at Jennifer Serravallo's *The Reading Strategies Book* and *The Writing Strategies Book*.

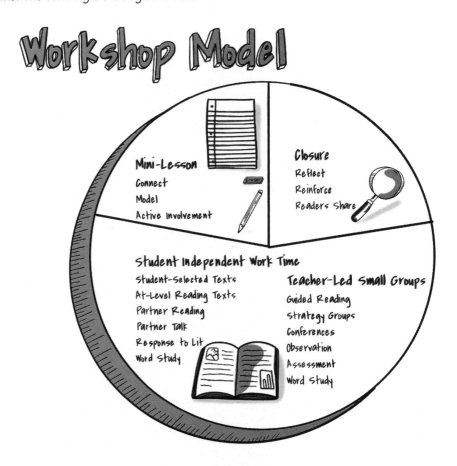

Podcasts

Podcasts are a great way to work on students' listening skills. You can teach students the power of the Pause button, so they can pause, rewind, and listen multiple times when listening on their own. You can also slow down the speed of most podcasts, which is especially useful for English learners.

When introducing podcasts to students, always make sure they read the short summary of the podcast. Give them enough time to figure out their paper position (landscape or portrait) and add their title to the paper to develop their sketchnote structure. Try to pick a short podcast, Listenwise.com is a great source for these short podcasts, but most on the site are for Grades 5–12. If you're using a longer podcast, find an appropriate place to pause after the first few minutes, then prompt students to go back and add to their sketchnote, or talk to an elbow partner about what each has in their sketchnote that the other is missing. Again, teach the power of the Pause button and remind them that they are in control when listening to podcasts; they can pause, rewind, and listen again.

A good podcast sketchnote should include:

- The speaker's name and a drawn representation of them.
- Names and drawings of other people that are introduced in the podcast.
- The main idea of the podcast (which should be prominent).
- A few key details.

Things that really help with podcasts are summarizing the content, using context clues, and asking questions in their sketchnote.

Read-Alouds

When you do a read-aloud, you should be stopping every few paragraphs or pages to ask questions or give prompts. The questions and prompts should guide the students to create their sketchnote. Their answers can be in the form of text, icons, and so on—all the things befitting a normal sketchnote—and use strategies to call the eye to the important details of the read-aloud passage, as prompted by the teacher. These could be questions like "What is the main idea of the passage so far?" or "Make three predictions about what happens in this passage." If the passage is particularly visual, prompt the students to draw what they see in their head at that moment. Utilizing elbow partners or table groups at sporadic times during the read-aloud can lead to richer sketchnotes.

Journal Prompts

Giving students time to write in their journals is always an important part of the writing process. Allowing time for students to develop a creative outlet to look at story ideas from the new perspective of using sketchnotes is a great way to cultivate bringing unexpected ideas to the surface. We have become a culture that can discern when something is "Instagram-worthy," but putting that same idea down in a journal or sketchnote takes some practice.

How do you tell your story?

Try asking students to think about times when they have taken out their cell phone to post to Instagram (or even ask students to physically get out their phone and look at their last few posts), and then to create a journal entry or a sketchnote about the story behind that post. If it is a food post, they could sketch a recipe. If it was a picture of friends, what were they doing with those friends? Ultimately, prompt them to think about the things that happen in their lives that an "audience" might want to hear about.

Another idea would be to prompt students with, "Draw out a story from a day in your life in a storyboard type manner. Tell us what is happening in a sequential order. Make the feelings and thoughts that are important to this story nice and big in a different font to help you potentially tell the story with richer detail later on. Add in little specific details to remind you of the important pieces of the story that make it all come together." Additionally, just sketchnoting a day from start to finish can be cathartic for students (and you, too) and produce less feelings of vulnerability than writing it out word for word.

The sketchnote itself could be a part of a longer journal entry or even an essay later on. Usually, the sooner you start a sketchnote in relation to the actual event the more details you will get into the sketch. There are online classes and books on this idea alone. *Draw Your Day* by Samantha Dion Baker is one of my favorites; scan the QR code on this page to see her daily journal entries on Instagram.

Draw Your Day

Think about your day yesterday or today. What did you do? How did you start your day? What places did you go? What chores or errands did you run? How did you end the day?

HEATHER HOXIE

4TH-GRADE TEACHER, OREGON
@MrsHoxie (Twitter)

Tapping into a range of learners and their various needs is essential, and sketchnotes provide one more option to do so. They allow students to show their understanding visually and to organize the information in a way that makes sense to them.

My favorite way to utilize sketchnoting is to focus on listening comprehension, which is often a difficult skill to teach. I find that using podcasts and videos really lifts the level of my students' comprehension, and they are able to retell the content in a more detailed, organized manner. First, students watch a *National Geographic* video or listen to a Brains On! podcast, which are some of my favorite resources (scan the QR codes for more information). We typically will do this as a whole class. Next, they sketchnote the key points on their own. Finally, they give both oral and written retells based on their visual notes, usually to their table group.

My biggest challenge with sketchnoting is the amount of pre-teaching that is necessary in order for students to sketchnote at a pace that is useable in the classroom. With elementary students, it is really important to model organizational structures, as well as when and why you might use the various

types. It is also important to teach some of the fundamental skills, such as bulleting, call outs, text styles, and so on. I found that it was much easier to spend time practicing these as skills, and then apply them in our work. When I modeled and encouraged quick ways to sketch, students were more successful in their own sketchnoting. I also recommend developing a class dictionary of the sketches and fonts that you have practiced. This reminds students of quick skills that they already know how to use.

National Geographic Videos

Brains On! Podcast

In particular, I found using sketchnotes to be particularly valuable in our informational text unit, which is a focused standard for fourth grade. As a class, we looked carefully at various ways that informational text is organized. Students then were able to connect these structures to their own sketchnotes. Students need practice looking at a text and determining the structure that the author is using. Utilizing sketchnotes has been a great way to look more deeply at text structure. Students not only are identifying the structure, but also are using organizational strategies in their note taking. These notes enhance their understanding of the content based on their knowledge of text structures.

CHAPTER 10

SKETCHNOTES IN MATH

Sketching and art skills aren't often associated with math lessons, but many elements of sketchnoting can actually be incorporated into math notes quite easily. Creating opportunities for sketchnoting during math lessons helps students synthesize key concepts; it may also help you hold the interest of students who ordinarily dread the analytical but favor artistic subjects. Color-coding strategies, using containers to draw your eye to key concepts or formulas, and adding in graphs and visuals for concepts are just some of the ways sketchnoting can enhance math notes. If you are taking notes from a textbook, remember to read through the current theory or topic and summarize it. If you have to show the steps of a formula, develop your own sequential method—meaning numbers, arrows, and colors to show your thinking. Show all the steps of an example, if you make a mistake, don't erase it; correct the mistake with another color and explain what you did wrong so you can remind yourself of that error (and not to make it again) when you study. For high school students, develop an icon or symbol to showcase AP (advanced placement) problems.

  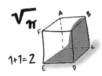

Discussing study tips for math notes also helps students think about how to put together their sketchnotes to facilitate the best study habits. For instance, a three-color system works well for math: Use blue for vocab and definitions, pink for key concepts, and orange to walk through equations or sample problems. Students should do as many practice problems as possible, so provide plenty of space in a sketchnote for problem practice.

Another way of having students practice sketchnotes in math is to provide a template, helping them to realize the important components of a math lecture. By providing them with a template that they still have to complete or fill in, you are at least providing students with a structure to start from. Gradually releasing them to create their own methods and structure without needing to use a teacher-created template, of course, is the ultimate goal. Once students do start creating their own sketchnotes without relying on a template, remind them that they should be leaving plenty of white space in a sketchnote as well, so that they have plenty of space to add more details, graphs or illustrations, or revisions when they go back and review for a test.

Students should also keep track of their questions: Sketchnotes won't help if you don't understand the content you are taking notes on! So make sure students write down their questions and, eventually, the answers to those questions. Answers could be put in a container or be added off to the side in the same color that students use consistently for questions. Whatever they do, just encourage students to keep track of and ask questions freely.

If students are taking notes in a math lecture they should focus only on the things that are being emphasized. Again, students should make note of any questions they have along the way. If there is anything that is covered in the lecture that isn't covered in the textbook, they should make sure to write it down and give it an icon or a different color. Anything written on the board is probably important and should be written down or, at the very least, thought of for the notes.

Giving students time to compare notes with someone else in class—even if they are not taking sketchnotes—is also very helpful. They should see what each other has, and they should add to their notes whatever is missing that they both agree was considered important during the lecture.

If a problem is being solved in class, remind students not to skip any steps in their notes; even if they know how to solve the problem in class, they might forget later on and need the detailed steps.

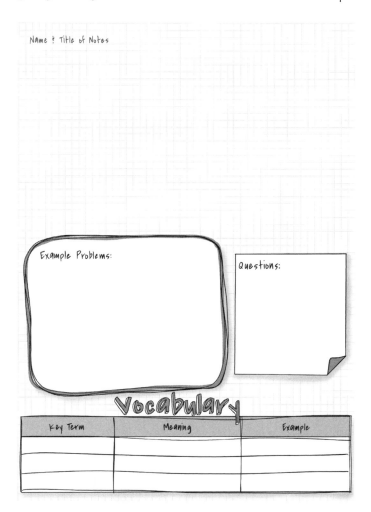

Sketchnote a Story Problem

Let's take a closer look at how you might introduce a story problem following the basic design of 3 Act Math by Dan Meyer. According to Meyer, when you are introducing a prompt for students to think and wonder about, the lesson itself might look like you can just wing it. In reality, however, it is very strategic, and sketchnote strategies used during the exploration will ultimately help students organize their thoughts better. Calling it Math 360, Ed Campos Jr. gets students up out of their seats to work on these problems at whiteboard spaces around the room, enabling students to collaborate and solve the

problems together. Whether students work on paper or on a whiteboard, sketchnote strategies, such as color coding, containers, connectors, symbols, and icons to illustrate points, will help with these notes.

Summary

GRADE LEVEL: 3-12

OBJECTIVE: Students will be introduced to a topic or idea through a prompt, they will then make predictions, collect data, and hopefully solve the problem. At the end of the lesson they should understand a strategy or solution to solve that problem and be able to reflect on their process to get there.

TIME ALLOTMENT: One hour or more, depending on the problem set's difficulty and how long students take to arrive at their answer.

Implementation

1. OPENER:

   a. Act 1: Present an image or video prompt, allow the students to take sketchnotes on the prompt. Ask them to write down things that they notice and wonder about. Tell them what your standard, learning target, or learning goal is for the day and how that problem relates.

   b. Have students make some estimates or predictions on the prompt in their notes, thinking about too high, too low, and best guess estimates. You are building up their own student agency here and level of wonder/inquiry in trying to solve the problem.

2. DIRECT INSTRUCTION:

Act 2: Ask the students to go back to their notes, but as a class ask the students what they need to solve the prompt.

a. Do they need measurements?

b. Do they need to look something up in order to solve it?

c. Do you as the teacher have information you can reveal and share with them to help them solve the problem?

3. INDEPENDENT WORK:

Give them time to collect data and solve the problem. This is the time you can work with them one on one, in small groups, or as a class to give them additional help in solving the problem.

4. CLOSING:

a. Act 3: Have students go over various strategies, and eventually reveal the answer to the problem. Have students explain their thinking, let them go back to their notes—highlight those notes for others to see by sharing through a document camera, tablet, or smartphone.

b. Have students reflect on their original estimates and predictions. Ask them what math they learned today. Having a specific idea of how students will do this reflection in class when they are setting up their notes (for instance, answering what math they learned today in a specific container) will help their study habits later on as they identify that concept and make it highly visible.

FOLLOW-UP ACTIVITIES

There are plenty of prompts already created out there on Dan Meyer's blog, or Graham Fletcher's website for elementary options. Scan the QR codes to explore new prompts.

Graham Fletcher   Dan Meyer

TIPS & TRICKS

- If students are struggling with the concept of taking notes during a 3 Act Math prompt, you could create a template for them to start and then gradually release them to make their own versions.

- Keeping in mind the important parts of each section: Their questions & predictions at the beginning, their estimates, the actual answer at the end, and their reflection on the learning.

Name & Title of Notes

Act 1: What do you think, what do you wonder about today's prompt?

Estimates: too high, too low, best guess.

Final Solution:

Reflection:

Vocab Review

Sometimes people gloss over the fact that there are a lot of new concepts and vocabulary words in a math class. Giving students the time and the skills to write down those words using sketchnote strategies is beneficial to all students, but primarily to those students that might not "get math." Using imagery, colors, and diagrams to illustrate math vocab and concepts can help make more connections for all students.

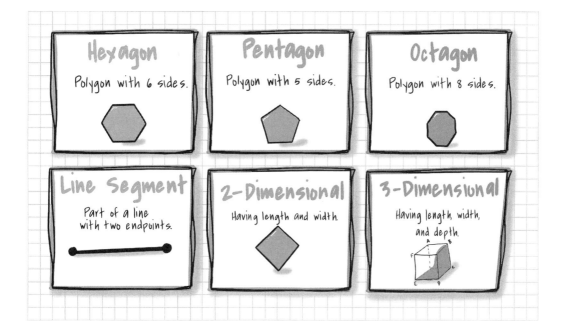

Creating a vocabulary page follows the same principles as any sketchnote: Students need a title based on the concept behind the vocabulary and information; as they begin to compile vocab words, concepts, and formulas related to that skill, they need to write them down. Show them multiple examples or ways to highlight the words and definitions. I typically use a word that is separated by a divider with the definition underneath it. Specific containers for vocab words or a color-code system could also be used. Students should additionally write down or draw the big ideas of that concept or word. If it needs to be illustrated in a graph, they should add one next to the word and definition.

Potentially these could be the same skills that students use for their typical lecture notes to draw their eye to the vocab terms. Having a whole sketchnote page in their notes for studying later would be a great tool for retention.

Explain a Formula or Current Content

Similar to creating a sketchnote devoted to just vocabulary terms, you could also create a page dedicated to formulas for a specific concept or skill. These sketchnotes should typically have the formula itself, a step-by-step guide to solving the formula, an illustration to explain the formula, and several color-coded example problems.

If for any reason there is a step that a student doesn't quite understand or that is still causing additional problems, have the student put a question mark or exclamation mark next to it. Call attention to it so that the student is aware of the issue when revisiting for studying later. For each step of the problem, suggest students write down in their own words an explanation of what they are doing. Really thinking about the structure of the notes here is important as well. Have students ask themselves: Do I like free-flowing "path" notes, or will a modular or column structure be helpful? An added tip would be to allow students to share and compare these notes with other students and the textbook to see if there is additional information that they could add to their notes that they missed the first time. With this in mind, suggest they leave space ahead of time or a dedicated section for items that might be added while comparing the notes.

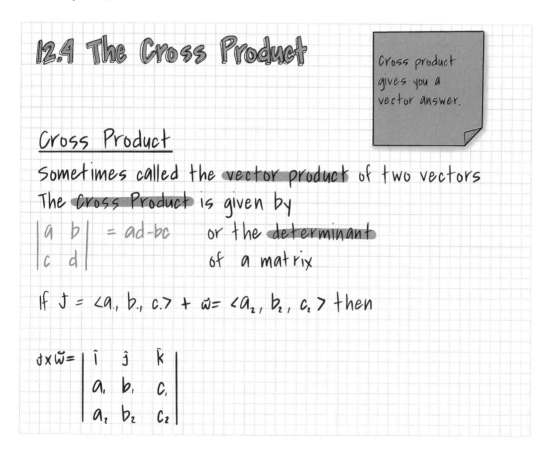

12.4 The Cross Product

Cross product gives you a vector answer.

Cross Product

Sometimes called the ~~vector product~~ of two vectors
The ~~Cross Product~~ is given by

$$\begin{vmatrix} a & b \\ c & d \end{vmatrix} = ad-bc \qquad \text{or the} ~~determinant~~$$
of a matrix

If $\vec{J} = \langle a_1, b_1, c_1 \rangle + \vec{w} = \langle a_2, b_2, c_2 \rangle$ then

$$\vec{J} \times \vec{w} = \begin{vmatrix} \hat{i} & \hat{j} & \hat{k} \\ a_1 & b_1 & c_1 \\ a_2 & b_2 & c_2 \end{vmatrix}$$

CYNTHIA NIXON

EDUCATIONAL TECHNOLOGY COACH, CALIFORNIA
@TeachingTechNix (Twitter, Voxer, and Instagram)

I am incredibly fortunate to be serving my K–12 school as an educational technology coach. My passion lies in helping students and teachers utilize technology in ways that allow for deeper learning. Prior to this position, I taught elementary school for nine years and specialized in mathematics instruction.

Sketchnotes are an incredibly powerful tool that can be used to increase your learning. I discovered them just as I was leaving the classroom and have used them exclusively for the last few years when taking notes.

The knowledge that drawing helps build connections isn't a new idea. What is one thing we almost always do when teaching reading vocabulary words? I'm sure you guessed it—have students draw a picture to represent the word. There are many places in our everyday teaching where this visual thinking can be extremely powerful, so it's frustrating that many educators are resistant to implement it in the classroom beyond vocabulary building. For example, math concepts can often be difficult for students to process without visual aids of some sort,

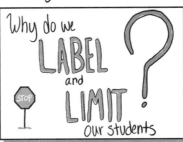

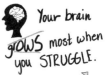

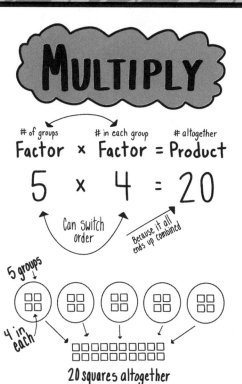

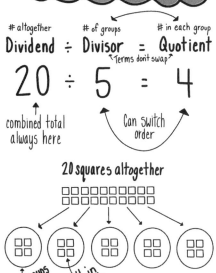

MULTIPLY

# of groups		# in each group		# altogether
Factor	×	Factor	=	Product
5	×	4	=	20

Can switch order

Because it all ends up combined

5 groups

4 in each

20 squares altogether

DIVIDE

# altogether		# of groups		# in each group
Dividend	÷	Divisor	=	Quotient

Terms don't swap

| 20 | ÷ | 5 | = | 4 |

combined total always here

Can switch order

20 squares altogether

5 groups

4 in each

@TEACHINGTECHNIX

so why not have them draw their own? When the students have to construct the visual, it takes more brain work, more connections are made, and students are much more likely to remember the information.

Many times, students are doing what I call The Digit Dance. They push the numbers around the page, following the steps that teachers demonstrated, and they normally get the right answers. But do they really get it? These students often can't tell if the answer is wrong just by looking at it, because they simply followed The Digit Dance to get that number. They have no conceptual basis on which to estimate a plausible answer. Allowing them some time to explore the concepts with visual thinking can not only help students grasp the concepts better, but also help students and

teachers spot those conceptual gaps before they get out of hand.

To understand sketchnoting's power, pick up your pen and give it a try yourself. Allow your creative juices to flow; you have them even if you think you don't. Trust me, I was the person who said I could never sketchnote because I wasn't an artist, but now I rely on sketchnotes and retain the content so much more than when I used to jot traditional notes. I even created a short video of my journey, which I hope you find inspiring. You can watch it on my blog (teachingtechnix.com) or by scanning the QR code.

CHAPTER 11

ASSESSMENT & EVALUATION

Grading students' notes can be a controversial topic. Notes are meant for students to use as a study tool, after all, not an assessment. Sketchnotes are valuable to the note taker because they hold meaning for the individual. I once was speaking to a group of new secondary teachers, and someone asked the question, how do I as a teacher grade something that has meaning and makes sense to the original note taker? The teacher was concerned about being able to read the student's handwriting and make meaning and sense out of a student's notes. My gut reaction was, why grade student notes? But as I do more reflection on this topic, I realize that I, too, graded notes in some capacity. So, this chapter will go over some tips and things to look for when, or if, you are going to be grading student sketchnotes.

Setting up Students for Success

When I first started heavily integrating technology, I began flipping my English class; having students take notes while they were watching the videos was a big component of that work. At the time, I remember reading a book about inclusivity in classrooms and having icons or markers as visual cues for students. Following that example, I began to include a pencil marker in my videos whenever I wanted the students to really focus on their notes and write down what I was going over. This proved to be incredibly helpful to all students. A few times when I used someone else's video instead of mine, the students immediately commented on how important that one visual cue had become to them. So, if you are having students take notes via flipped classroom videos or live during a lecture, this is one tip to be strategic about: Place an icon where you know there are key details or main ideas that you need the students to include in their notes. Those key details or main ideas could be things that you look for when you are grading or providing feedback on notes. For example, as I walked from desk to desk I would be able to quickly scan students notes, not for *all* the content but to look for those most important items. If students are using proper note hierarchy, containers, color coding, or connectors, your icon-highlighted key points should be easily seen and identified.

clear message
of main ideas

text and images

Subtitles quotes
Titles ~~vocab~~

containers
and connectors

a good sketchnote

To be successful, sometimes students need to see models and templates that they can build on when later developing their own version of sketchnoting a topic or lesson. Ultimately, giving students too much information can lead to lost content—especially when students have to take in the new content and process it, while at the same time trying to restructure it into a sketchnote. Students need processing time. The point of good note taking is to allow students to process the new information in a way that is meaningful to them. If you notice students struggling to come up with their own structure for a sketchnote, a template could be helpful. As you have heard from multiple educators, helping students develop a visual vocabulary for the content is another useful strategy. Sketchnotes allow students to make connections and synthesize the information, which is why note taking, and sketchnotes in particular, is so powerful. We just have to provide some of the tools to help them get underway if it isn't coming innately.

Quick Grading Tips & Tricks

Another tip for grading sketchnotes is to simply walk around the class at the beginning of the period with your gradebook and jot down each student's grade. I use a PDF of my seating chart in a note taking app on my iPad and record a grade in the participation category, which is weighted a very low 10% of their actual grade. I always look for the title, the key points in their notes, a summary of the content, and a question they asked about their learning. I give them 7/10 points if they just took notes and I can see a few key details clearly marked. They get 8/10 points if they asked a question but didn't do their summary. They get 10/10 if they did their notes, asked a question, and did a fairly good-sized summary. Writing this score down in your gradebook and providing students with quick formative feedback is great for both you and your students.

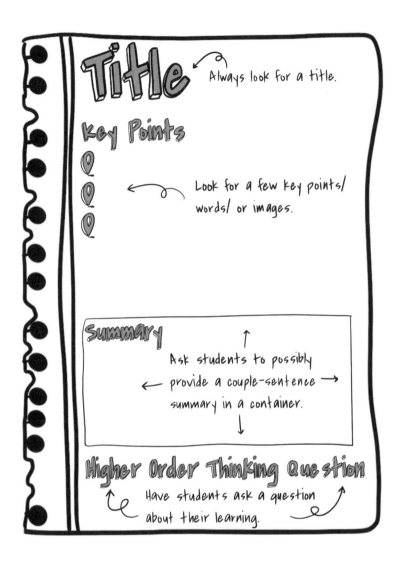

At the very beginning of the year, I set up my note-taking expectations for students: We take notes together as a class, and I show them my expectations and also teach them the power of the Pause button (as discussed in Chapter 9). When I notice that students aren't meeting my standards, by neglecting a summary, for example, we go back and workshop the relevant points quite a bit throughout the year. Modeling and expectations from the beginning are so important.

Feedback from Structure & Partner Work

Another thing you could focus on is the structure of their notes. I know I am continuously working on the structure of my own sketchnotes. Structure helps with reading and studying the content later, but it also helps convey a student's understanding. As they get better and better at the skill of sketchnoting, their structures improve and can change depending on the content of the sketchnote. Again, modeling structure expectations at the beginning, and even providing templates, can help build this skill. Additionally, having one-on-one feedback with students that are struggling with structure, perhaps during a conferring session if you run a workshop model, would be extremely helpful for a student. Ultimately, sketchnotes are a tool to be studied and used by the note takers themselves. It isn't about making the sketchnote more readable for you, as the teacher grading the sketchnote, it is about making it more clear and concise for the student to use later. Are they showing their connections? Do they need to clean up and clarify the content? Can the student easily tell you what is happening in their sketchnote?

Turning and sharing sketchnotes with an elbow partner is another great tool to help in cleaning up sketchnotes, both in structure but also in the content. Seeing how other students structured their notes, how they conveyed meaning with a topic, the pieces of info that they picked out as key details, and recognizing and learning from these differences—this act will force students to refine their skills of synthesizing the information. It is more critical feedback than just getting an 8/10 on a paper, even if the students don't realize it.

CLASSROOM VOICES
MISTY KLUESNER

DIGITAL INNOVATION TEACHER ON SPECIAL ASSIGNMENT, CALIFORNIA
@MistyKluesner (Twitter and Instagram)

The big idea of sketchnotes is that it is a method of making your thinking visual. Sometimes our thinking will be with words and sometimes with pictures (and most times, it will be both). The idea is that we are taking advantage of both worlds and creating something tangible that we can reference later and perhaps share with others.

Sketchnotes are personal: How I connect to and visualize something will be different than how others do. That is why they are so powerful; they allow us to infuse our notes with personal meaning, creating connections that are more powerful than with traditional note taking.

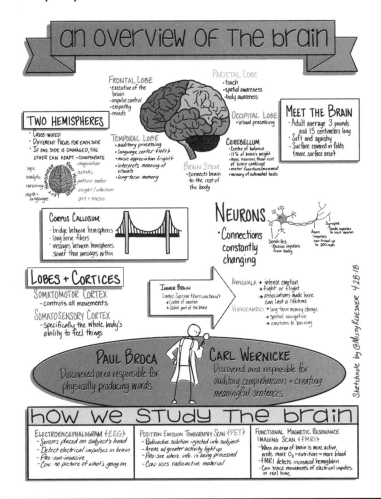

My biggest challenge with sketchnotes in the classroom has been guiding students to think critically about information and focusing on capturing the big ideas. Most students will try to capture every single piece of information that they hear or read, which makes sketchnoting really challenging—that's a lot of information to record.

I find that the best way to get comfortable with creating images that show your thinking is to practice often. One way is to just create a 5-minute doodle inspired by a word or prompt each day. (This is a great exercise for students, too.) By drawing daily (or as often as you can), you are able to build confidence in your abilities, as well as strengthen the practice of connecting abstract concepts and ideas to concrete images. The 5-minute time limit helps ensure that you don't get caught up in being a perfectionist and enables you to practice getting ideas from your head to paper quickly, which is especially crucial for live sketchnoting.

JOIN AN ONLINE COMMUNITY

To build a sketchnoting culture in your classroom with your students, you must be willing to sketchnote and doodle *with* your students. You must gain confidence in the act of sketchnoting, and the only way to do that is to practice. In addition to the ideas we've discussed, the Internet is full of resources, daily and weekly prompts, hashtags and people to follow, and step-by-step guides to help you.

Coffee Shop Sketchnote

Take yourself to a coffee shop, draw the people you see, the conversations you hear. The cup of your coffee or tea. Time to start getting in the habit of drawing live.

Online Challenges & Prompts

From Twitter to Instagram and beyond, you can find challenges to try, ways to share your work, and opportunities to get involved with an online sketchnoting community. An online community can be a consistent source of inspiration and feedback to keep you going. Sharing your work with your peers online can also help you let go of your adult "I can't draw" attitude. Over the last couple of years, I have had quite a few starts and stops, but joining an online challenge or seeing someone else creating always motivates me to want to create as well.

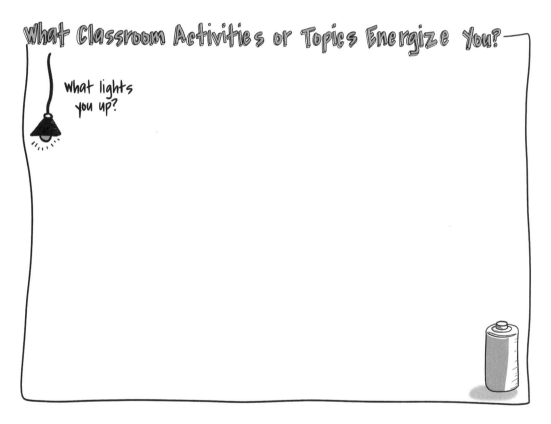

What Classroom Activities or Topics Energize You?

what lights you up?

Benefits

Sending the good, the bad, and the ugly out into the world for others to give you feedback on can be difficult, but you can learn much more from a thoughtful critique than from polite, empty praise. This clearly takes a growth mindset, but by showing your students that you are comfortable attempting and sharing a possibly horrible drawing for others to comment on, you will develop the sketchnote culture in your classroom.

Remember, and remind your students, that what matters is whether a doodle makes sense to *you*, the creator, and *your* brain. You aren't creating art; sketchnoting is a process for processing information and retaining that content. Eventually, with more practice, your efforts might become more artistic, but that shouldn't be the ultimate goal any more than lack of artistry should be a roadblock to begin.

Ultimately, by sharing with a larger community, whether that is online or with your classroom, you are opening yourself up to the possibility of improving your sketchnotes, as well as your information processing, and overall understanding. Additionally, because people process images as information more easily and quickly, sharing sketchnotes is a way to highlight information that matters to you or what you are currently learning. Who knows, you could be the source of inspiration for someone else to start sketchnoting.

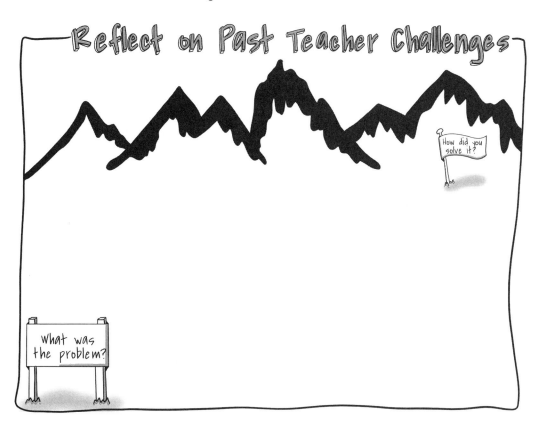

One of the easiest ways to get started is to share a picture of your work on Twitter or Instagram using one or more of the following hashtags. To save time, I keep my most used hashtags in a note in my phone's Notes app, then paste the ones I need into my social media posts!

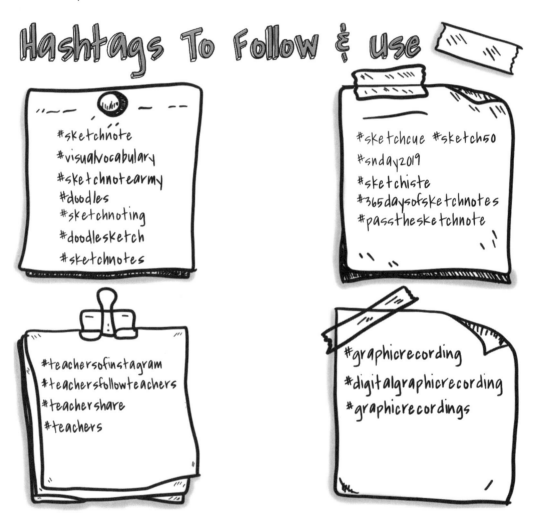

Hashtags To Follow & Use

#sketchnote
#visualvocabulary
#sketchnotearmy
#doodles
#sketchnoting
#doodlesketch
#sketchnotes

#sketchcue #sketch50
#snday2019
#sketchiste
#365daysofsketchnotes
#passthesketchnote

#teachersofinstagram
#teachersfollowteachers
#teachershare
#teachers

#graphicrecording
#digitalgraphicrecording
#graphicrecordings

Resources

Once you are ready to move beyond maybe just posting one or two sketchnotes sporadically, the next best thing is to join a challenge via social media.

On Instagram you can find a ton of doodle and lettering challenges to get you started practicing and improving your sketchnoting basics. One of my favorites is Apsi's (@thedoodleguide) *52-Week Challenge*: Each week she provides a prompt for you to sketchnote a page, using such themes as expressions, faces, or hands. If you just need a single prompt to guide you, this is a great way to get started. Another popular example, @hollypixels provides daily *Draw and Letter Prompts*, which are usually centered around a monthly theme. For even more options, check out the Instagram account @letteringchallengehq for constant updates on many monthly lettering challenges.

Drawing Challenges

#doodlechallenge #dailydoodles
#letteringchallenge #drawingprompts
#letteringprompts #hollypixels #dailylettering
#dailydrawing #dailydoodle #doodleaday
#doodlelessons #doodlewithdiane
#doodleinstitute #howtodoodle
#oodlesofdoodle-challenge___
(put the month code at the end)
#mydoodlenine
(smaller more manageable monthly challenge)
#52weekvisualvocabulary

Another option is to try one of the teacher-run challenges. For example, *Pass the Sketchnote* is a nice, easy opportunity to join an international group of sketchnoters. Monica Spillman (@mospillman) and Carrie Baughcum (@heckawesome) usually run the challenge once or twice a year. You can always count on one of those instances being on World Sketchnote Day, which is in mid-January. You can sign up through Twitter; follow the hashtag #passthesketchnote for updates. When you sign up you are attached to other participants in different time zones and given a theme. The first person in the team begins a sketchnote, then passes it off to the next person in the group to add to it, and so on. It is a lot of fun, and you could easily try a variation of this idea within your classroom or school, as well!

Two annual challenges are *#sketchCUE* and *#sketch50*. In the month leading up to the Spring CUE conference, which showcases innovation and technology in education (cue.org/spring), you can find daily prompts announced via Twitter by following the hashtag #sketchCUE. Cate Tolnai (@CateTolnai), Wanda Terral (@wterral), and Cynthia Nixon (@TeachingTechNix) helped start #sketchCUE. Almost immediately following #sketchCUE, the #sketch50 challenge usually occurs at the end of March and consists of fifty days of prompts leading up to the ISTE Conference & Expo in June. You can find out more about #sketch50, and even use previous prompts and resources to get a jump start, at www.sketch50.org.

People to Follow

My favorite place to get inspiration and see what other sketchnoters are doing is Instagram. Twitter has some interesting conversations, but because Instagram is a visual medium, it lends itself a little better to sketchnotes and graphic recording. Scan the QR codes below to see updated resources from most social media platforms.

Instagram
Accounts to Follow

Twitter
Accounts to Follow

YouTube Channels
to Subscribe to

Websites and
Online Resources

Go Practice Sketchnotes

By now, you have practiced a great deal, and you are ready for the next step. This is a call to action: Make a commitment to follow some sketchnoters or hashtags and/or participate in an upcoming challenge. Announce your intention in the space provided on the next page.

Call To Action

JOIN AN ONLINE COMMUNITY

Wow! That was a lot of information!

I know when I first started seeing people sketchnoting a few years ago it really spoke to me, it made sense to my brain, and I knew I wanted to learn and try it for myself. I don't think I started down this path with the intention of writing a book, but I definitely wanted to learn and bring it back to the classrooms in my school district. I read whatever I could get my hands on; most did not pertain to the classroom teacher or student. And I practiced. I practiced a lot. I am still practicing, and I am teaching the skills that have helped me to anyone that will listen.

Remember to keep your drawings simple, build on your skills, and you will create your own style. Let go of judgment and be okay to make mistakes and try new things—this is so important to highlight for your students. Share your sketchnotes with your classroom and with others online. I am so excited you have started on this journey, and I hope you find joy and fun in creating notes just like I have.

REFERENCES

Academic Center for Excellence. (n.d.). *Note taking tips for math.* Retrieved from
www.aims.edu/fye/docs/learn/note-taking-math.pdf

Adams, M. (2016, October 19). Here's the best note-taking strategies for each
type of class. *Scholarship Points.* Retrieved from www.scholarshippoints.com/
campuslife/heres-the-best-note-taking-strategies-for-each-type-of-class

Baker, S. D. (2018). *Draw your day: An inspiring guide to keeping a sketch journal.*
California: Watson-Guptill.

Bell, J. (2018, September 6). *Teaching current events in the history classroom.*
Retrieved from www.middleweb.com/38641/teaching-current-events-in-
the-history-classroom

Berick, J. H., & Turk Berick, C. (n.d.). Effective Note-taking in Lectures. Retrieved
from https://www.cc-seas.columbia.edu/node/31875

Blakemore, E. (2018, September 12). 73,000-year-old doodle may be world's
oldest drawing. *National Geographic.* Retrieved from www.nationalgeographic.
com/science/2018/09/news-ancient-humans-art-hashtag-ochre-south-
africa-archaeology

Bormann, J., & Burgess, D. (2017). *Professionally driven: Empower every educator to
redefine PD.* New Berlin, WI: The Bretzmann Group.

Bosch, K. (2014, October 28). Predicting weather sketchnotes by 4th grade
[Blog post]. *Technology from SCS Elementary.* Retrieved from
blogs.southfieldchristian.org/elemapptitude/predicting-weather-
sketchnotes-by-4th-grade

Bosch, K. (2015, February 6). Student sketchnotes across subject areas
[Blog post]. *The Middle Pages.* Retrieved from blogs.southfieldchristian.org/
middlepages/2015/02/sketchnotes-across-subject-areas

Bosch, K. (2015, September 27). Journal sketchnotes [Blog post]. *The Middle Pages*. Retrieved from blogs.southfieldchristian.org/middlepages/2015/09/journal-sketchnotes

Bosch, K. (2016, September 26). Sketchnoting—"how to" sketchnotes [Blog post]. *The Middle Pages*. Retrieved from blogs.southfieldchristian.org/middlepages/2016/09/sketchnoting-how-to-sketchnotes

Brown, S. (2015). *The doodle revolution: Unlock the power to think differently*. New York: Portfolio Penguin.

Carey, K. (n.d.). Cornell notes [Blog post]. *Math Strategies*. Retrieved from mathematicstrategies.weebly.com/cornell-notes.html

CBS News [CBS Sunday Morning]. (2014, June 22). *The higher purpose of doodling* [Video file]. Retrieved from www.youtube.com/watch?v=4uaSlM1BAa8

Chamorro-Premuzic, T. (2015, February 23). You can teach someone to be more creative. *Harvard Business Review*. Retrieved from hbr.org/2015/02/you-can-teach-someone-to-be-more-creative

Croxall, B. (2010, May 5). How to grade students' class participation. *The Chronicle of Higher Education*. Retrieved from www.chronicle.com/blogs/profhacker/how-to-grade-students-class-participation/23726

Dawkins, P. (2017, November 18). *Taking notes*. Retrieved from tutorial.math.lamar.edu/Extras/StudyMath/TakingNotes.aspx

Delfin, C. (2012, January 7). *Sketcho frenzy: The basics of visual note-taking* [Video file]. Retrieved from www.youtube.com/watch?v=gY9KdRfNN9w&t=25s

Delfin, C. (2012, January 2). *Sketcho frenzy: Pie chart* [Video file]. Retrieved from www.youtube.com/watch?v=pyCVGaNW54U&t=14s

Delfin, C. (2012, January 2). *Sketcho frenzy: Venn diagram* [Video file]. Retrieved from www.youtube.com/watch?v=dTPe4XmVzOc

Durand, P. (2011, February 4). *The history of graphic facilitation (time lapse scribing)* [Video file]. Retrieved from alphachimp.com/video/the-history-of-graphic-facilitation-time-lapse-scribing.html

English Teaching Forum & Global Publishing Solutions. (2016). *Try this: Current events.* Retrieved from americanenglish.state.gov/files/ae/resource_files/ forum_current_events.pdf

Ferlazzo, L. (2018, March 15). Active listening: Using times videos, podcasts and articles to practice a key skill. *The New York Times.* Retrieved from www.nytimes.com/ 2018/03/15/learning/lesson-plans/active-listening-using-times-videos-podcasts-and-articles-to-practice-a-key-skill.html

Fleming, G. (2019, January 30). *How to take math notes with a smartpen.* Retrieved from www.thoughtco.com/taking-math-notes-1857214

Fletcher, G. (2018, October 11). *3-act tasks.* Retrieved from gfletchy.com/ 3-act-lessons

Fryer, W. (2018, November 25). *Visual notetaking.* Retrieved from showwithmedia.com/ visual-notetaking

Gammill, D. (2016, January 6). The benefits of using doodling and sketchnotes in the classroom. *Education Week Teacher.* Retrieved from www.edweek.org/tm/ articles/2016/01/04/the-benefits-of-using-doodling-and-sketchnotes.html

Gardner, T. (n.d.). *Plot structure: A literary elements mini-lesson.* ReadWriteThink. Retrieved from www.readwritethink.org/classroom-resources/lesson-plans/ plot-structure-literary-elements-904.html?tab=4 - tabs

Gerstein, J. (2012, September 4). Visual note-taking [Blog post]. *User Generated Education.* Retrieved from usergeneratededucation.wordpress.com/2012/ 09/04/visual-note-taking

Herting, N., & Willems, H. (2016). *Draw your big idea: The ultimate creativity tool for turning thoughts into action and dreams into reality!* San Francisco, CA: Chronicle Books.

Hollowell, K. (2017, November 21). How to take notes from a social studies textbook. *Seattle pi.* Retrieved from education.seattlepi.com/notes-social-studies-textbook-2585.html

IB like Cole. (2018, February 28). *Every IB biology drawing you need to know* [Video file]. Retrieved from www.youtube.com/watch?v=Npb42kiqj8A&feature=youtu.be

Illinois Institute of Technology. (2009). *General science lab note taking*. Retrieved from sciencefair.math.iit.edu/analysis/sciencelabnote

International Society for Technology in Education. (2016). *ISTE standards for students*. Retrieved from www.iste.org/standards/for-students

International Society for Technology in Education. (2017). *ISTE standards for educators*. Retrieved from www.iste.org/standards/for-educators

Johnson, B. (2015, November 24). Creative ways to grade and provide feedback for students. *Edutopia*. Retrieved from www.edutopia.org/blog/creative-ways-grade-and-provide-feedback-students-ben-johnson

Keller, I. (n.d.). *Geometry vocab terms!* Retrieved from www.teacherspayteachers.com/Product/Geometry-Vocab-Terms-FREEBIE-2451945

KMPapple. (n.d.). *Math: Printable geometry vocabulary cards: Grades 2–5*. Retrieved from www.teacherspayteachers.com/Product/Math-Printable-Geometry-Vocabulary-Cards-Grades-2-5-292193

Kristy42100. (2016, December 5). *Solving number stories using start/change/end template* [Video file]. Retrieved from www.youtube.com/watch?v=oujxlx2IBXQ

Kruse, M. (2018, June 24). Note taking strategies and tips for secondary [Blog post]. *Reading and Writing Haven*. Retrieved from www.readingandwritinghaven.com/note-taking-strategies-and-tips-for-secondary

Kuepper-Tetzel, C. (2018, March 29). A note on note-taking [Blog post]. *The Learning Scientists*. Retrieved from www.learningscientists.org/blog/2018/3/29-1

Lee, D. (2018). *Design thinking in the classroom: Easy-to-use teaching tools to foster creativity, encourage innovation and unleash potential in every student*. Berkeley, CA: Ulysses Press.

Literacy & Math Ideas. (2014, September 12). Note taking in math [Blog post]. Retrieved from literacymathideas.blogspot.com/2014/09/note-taking-in-math.html

Little Lady. (2017, June 12). *Fun history note taking tips* [Video file]. Retrieved from www.youtube.com/watch?v=KZTR27egC7Y

Math Giraffe. (2018, June 5). Sketch notes vs. doodle notes [Blog post]. *Math Giraffe*. Retrieved from www.mathgiraffe.com/blog/sketch-notes-vs-doodle-notes

McKay, B., & McKay, K. (2019, January 31). *Write this down: Note-taking strategies for academic success*. Retrieved from www.artofmanliness.com/articles/write-this-down-note-taking-strategies-for-academic-success

Meyer, D. (2013, May 8). *Teaching with three-act tasks: Act one* [Blog post]. *dy/dan*. Retrieved from blog.mrmeyer.com/2013/teaching-with-three-act-tasks-act-one

Millin, S. (2016, May 25). Using podcasts to develop listening skills [Blog post]. *Teaching English*. Retrieved from www.teachingenglish.org.uk/blogs/sandymillin/using-podcasts-develop-listening-skills

Moran, K. (2017, February 7). *8 smart ways to teach current events in the classroom in 2017*. Retrieved from www.weareteachers.com/current-events-classroom

Mosca, J. F., & Rieley, D. (2017). *The girl who thought in pictures: The story of Dr. Temple Grandin*. Seattle, WA: The Innovation Press.

Mueller, P. A., & Oppenheimer, D. M. (2014). The pen is mightier than the keyboard: Advantages of longhand over laptop note taking. *Psychological Science, 25*(6), 1159–1168. doi.org/10.1177/0956797614524581

National Council of Teachers of English & International Reading Association. (2012). *NCTE/IRA standards for the English language arts*. Retrieved from www.ncte.org/standards/ncte-ira

National Education Association. (n.d.). An educator's guide to the "four Cs." Retrieved from www.nea.org/tools/52217.htm

National Governors Association Center for Best Practices & Council of Chief State School Officers. (2010). *Common core state standards for English language arts*. Retrieved from corestandards.org/ELA-Literacy

Neill, D. (n.d.). *Verbal to visual*. Retrieved from www.verbaltovisual.com

Norris, C., & Soloway, E. (2017, May 8). Picting, not writing, is the literacy of today's youth. *THE Journal*. Retrieved from thejournal.com/articles/2017/05/08/picting-not-writing.aspx

Oxford Learning. (2017, May 3). *How to take study notes: 5 effective note taking methods.* Retrieved from www.oxfordlearning.com/5-effective-note-taking-methods

Perry, K., Bell, M. A., & Weimar, H. (2018). *Sketchnoting in school: Discover the benefits (and fun) of visual note taking.* Lanham, MD: Rowman & Littlefield.

Pillars, W. (2016). *Visual note-taking for educators: A teacher's guide to student creativity.* New York, NY: W.W. Norton & Company.

Pink, D. H. (2012). *A whole new mind: Why right-brainers will rule the future.* New York, NY: Riverhead Books.

Pistrui, J. (2018, January 18). The future of human work is imagination, creativity, and strategy. *Harvard Business Review.* Retrieved from hbr.org/2018/01/the-future-of-human-work-is-imagination-creativity-and-strategy

Ramirez, A. (2017, August 28). The lowdown on longhand. *Edutopia.* Retrieved from www.edutopia.org/blog/writing-by-hand-benefits-brain-ainissa-ramirez

Reif, C. (2015, August 21). *Getting practical: 3 ways writers can use sketchnotes* [Blog post]. *Cheryl Reif Writes.* Retrieved February 5, 2019, from www.cherylreif.com/2015/03/26/getting-practical-3-ways-writers-can-use-sketchnotes

Roam, D. (2012). *Blah blah blah: What to do when words don't work.* New York, NY: Portfolio.

Rohde, M. (2012). *The sketchnote handbook.* Berkeley, CA: Pearson Education.

Rohde, M. (2013, June 3). Sketchnotes in history class with Brent Pillsbury [Blog post]. *Sketchnote Army.* Retrieved from sketchnotearmy.com/blog/2013/6/3/sketchnotes-in-history-class-with-brent-pillsbury.html

Rohde, M. (2018, March 17). *Sketchnotes for thinking things through.* Retrieved from rohdesign.com/weblog/category/sketchnotes

Royal Society for the Encouragement of Arts, Manufactures and Commerce. [The RSA]. (2010, April 1). *RSA animate: Drive: The surprising truth about what motivates us* [Video file].Retrieved from www.youtube.com/watch?v=u6XAPnuFjJc

Royal Society for the Encouragement of Arts, Manufactures and Commerce. [The RSA]. (2010, October 14). *RSA animate: Changing education paradigms* [Video file]. Retrieved from www.youtube.com/watch?v=zDZFcDGpL4U

Schrock, K. (2018, November 13). *Sketchnoting in education*. Retrieved from www.schrockguide.net/sketchnoting.html

Schwartz, K. (2016, June 3). Making learning visible: Doodling helps memories stick. *MindShift*. Retrieved from www.kqed.org/mindshift/39941/ making-learning-visible-doodling-helps-memories-stick

Specktor, B. (n.d.). 6 ways doodling can make you smarter, happier, and more productive. *Reader's Digest*. Retrieved from www.rd.com/advice/work-career/ doodling-benefits/?platform=hootsuite

Spencer, B. (2014, August 19). What your child's drawings say about their IQ: How the sketches a kid makes at age four point to teenage intelligence. *Daily Mail*. Retrieved from www.dailymail.co.uk/sciencetech/article-2728381/ How-child-s-drawings-four-clue-cleverness-Young-depict-human-form-artworks-likely-brighter-teenage-years.html

Statics and Stationery. (2015, August 27). *How to take notes: From a math lecture* [Video file]. Retrieved from www.youtube.com/watch?v=iX64YC5jcVQ

Stencel, J. E. (2001). Note-taking techniques in the science classroom: Focusing on the important concepts in science. *Journal of College Science Teaching, 30*(6), 403–405.

Studyign. (2015, November 4). *How to take math lecture notes* [Video file]. Retrieved from www.youtube.com/watch?v=OE7BbqUNOHO

Studyquill. (2017, December 18). *How to take history notes* [Video file]. Retrieved from www.youtube.com/watch?v=kbDRTtof5ko

Teaching Channel. (2018, June 27). *Post-its: Little notes for big discussions* [Video File]. Retrieved from www.teachingchannel.org/video/enhance-student-note-taking

TED. (2015, February 5). *Tom Wujec: Got a wicked problem? First, tell me how you make toast* [Video file]. Retrieved www.youtube.com/watch?v=_vS_b7cJn2A

TEDx. (2012, August 31). *Drawing in class: Rachel Smith at TEDxUFM* [Video file]. Retrieved from www.youtube.com/watch?v=3tJPeumHNLY

Thompson, V. (2016, September 29). Note taking tips for science class. *Seattle pi.* Retrieved from education.seattlepi.com/taking-tips-science-class-1682.html

Toku, M. (n.d.). *Children's artistic and aesthetic development: The influence of pop-culture in children's drawings.* Retrieved from www.csuchico.edu/~mtoku/vc/Articles/toku/Study1.htm

Toselli, M. (2016, September 19). Explain history and economics with sketchnotes: Gary Goodwin [Blog post]. *Sketchnote Army.* Retrieved from sketchnotearmy.com/blog/2016/9/19/explain-history-and-economics-with-sketchnotes-gary-goodwin.html

University of Iowa. (n.d.). *Taking lecture notes: History.* Retrieved from clas.uiowa.edu/history/teaching-and-writing-center/guides/taking-lecture-notes

WikiHow. (2018, November 26). *How to write social studies notes.* Retrieved January 11, 2019 from www.wikihow.com/Write-Social-Studies-Notes

WikiHow. (2018, September 9). *How to take notes for science.* Retrieved February 9, 2019, from www.wikihow.com/Take-Notes-for-Science

WikiHow. (2019, February 6). *How to take perfect math notes.* Retrieved January 11, 2019, from www.wikihow.com/Take-Perfect-Math-Notes

Wujec, T. (n.d.). *Draw how to make toast.* Retrieved from www.drawtoast.com

INDEX

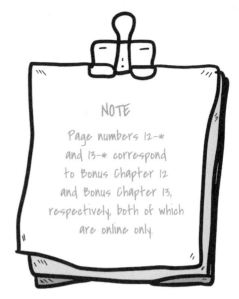

NOTE

Page numbers 12-* and 13-* correspond to Bonus Chapter 12 and Bonus Chapter 13, respectively, both of which are online only.

Numbers

2-dimensional sketchnote, 129
3 Act Math, 124
3 Knowledge Constructor, ISTE (International Society for Technology in Education) Standards, 25
3-dimensional sketchnote, 129
4 Cs of 21st Century Learning, 74–76
4 steps of learning, 16
6 Creative Communicator Standard, 26
6 Facilitator Standard, 24
6 Types of Meetings sketchnote, *13-10*
8 Writing Common Core State Standard, 28
10-second timer, QR code, 10
52-Week Challenge, 147
2022 Skills Outlook sketchnote, *12-3*

A

accessories, adding to figures, 41–42
active listening, practicing, 71
activity, retention of experience, 20
Adobe Illustrator Draw app, 59–60
Adonit products
    Jot Pro stylus, 60
    Pro app, 62
age, signifying in drawings, 39–40
analog tools, 57–59, 64–65
Android devices, 59
animating stick figures, 42
annotating and highlighting, 68–69, 93, 107
Apple Pencil, 59, 62
apps, using, 59–62
Apsi's *52-Week Challenge*, 147
arrows, using to connect ideas, 49, 73
assessment and evaluation
    feedback from structure/partner work, 139
    quick grading tips and tricks, 137–138
    tips for success, 135–137
audience, engaging, 18
auditory learning, 15
AWW App, 59, 61

B

banners and containers, 50–51
Baughcum, Carrie, 8, 147
Best Practice for Multilingual sketchnote, 102
Bittel, Jason, 95
Blah Blah Blah: What to Do When Words Don't Work, 69–70
board meetings, 1970s, 6
body shapes, thinking about, 43
bold text, 47
Bonus Chapter 12
    2022 Skills Outlook sketchnote, *12-3*
    design thinking explanation, *12-9*
    design thinking process, *12-8*, *12-9*
    design thinking sketchnote, *12-4*
    Empathy Interview-Understand Your User, *12-11*
    Genius Hour Project Timeline, *12-5*
    Herrera, Manuel S., *12-12*, *12-13*
    inquiry-driven learning, *12-4*
    interviews, *12-10*
    PBL (project-based learning), *12-4*
    Peer Interview-What Is Your Teacher Legacy?, *12-8*
    project timelines, *12-5*, *12-6*, *12-7*
    STEAM (Science, Technology, Engineering, Arts, Mathematics), *12-4*
    Visual Thinking sketchnote, *12-12*
Bonus Chapter 13
    6 Types of Meetings sketchnote, *13-10*
    lesson planning and creativity, *13-3*, *13-4*, *13-5*
    New Bloom's Taxonomy, *13-3*
    Risk Taker sketchnote, *13-5*
    strategies for books, *13-6*

strategies for conferences, *13-7, 13-8, 13-9*
strategies for department meetings, *13-9, 13-10*
strategies for staff meetings, *13-9, 13-10*
book, drawing, 37
book strategies, *13-6*
brain
    4 steps of learning, 16
    deeper learning connections, 15
    overview sketchnote, 140
Brains On! podcast, 118
Brown, Sunni, 11, *13-9*, 24
bullets, using with text, 32

C

calculator, drawing, 37
Campos, Ed, 124
captions, using with text, 32
categorization/focus/synthesis, 32
cause and effect, social studies, 101
cave/rock paintings, 6
classroom note taking. *See* note taking
climax, ELA (English Language Acquisition), 108
Coffee Shop sketchnote, 142
collaboration, 74–76
color
    highlighting, 93
    thinking about, 57–58
Common Core State Standards, 23, 28
communication, 26, 74–75
comprehending text, 15
Computer Science Pilot Program drawing, 46
conference strategies, *13-7, 13-8, 13-9*
confidence, providing, 57
connecting ideas, 49
containers and banners, 50–51
content
    interpreting, 71
    understanding, 19
convection currents, 91
Cornell notes, 68
Creative Communicator Standard, 26
creativity, 74–75
critical thinking, 74–75
The Cross Product, math sketchnote, 131
cup, drawing, 11
Curl, Bettina, 104–105
current events, social studies, 94–98

D

deeper learning connections, 15
department meeting strategies, *13-9, 13-10*
depth and dimensionality, implying, 43
design thinking
    explanation, *12-9*
    intro to, 30
    process, *12-8, 12-9*
    sketchnote, *12-4*
digital resources, 63
digital tools, 59–62
Dion Baker, Samantha, 116
Divide sketchnote, 133
dividers, using with titles, 49–50
Doodle Buddy app, 60
doodle game, playing, 9–13
The Doodle Revolution, *13-9*, 24
doodling
    challenges on Instagram, 147
    encouraging, 58, 141
Draw and Letter Prompts, 147
Draw Your Day, 116–117
drawing. *See also* illustrations; sketchnotes
    apps, 59
    banners, 51
    Computer Science Pilot Program, 46
    cup, 11
    environments, 41
    eyebrows, 39
    human figures, 41
    icons or images, 10–11, 38
    items, 37
    laptops, 40
    mouths, 39
    My Day, 45
    noses, 42
    Passages, 46
    people, 39–44
    phones, 11, 40
    practicing, 8
    process of making toast, 29–31
    Social Studies in BSD, 46
    stick figures, 41
    symbol or icon for *life*, 12
    tadpole, 41
Drawing Challenges sketchnote, 147
drop shadow, 43
Dual Coding Theory, 17–19
Dual Language sketchnote, 102. *See also* ELA (English
    Language Acquisition); language acquisition
Duckworth, Sylvia, 6

E

educators, ISTE Standards (6 Facilitator), 24
edu-sketching, 6
ELA (English Language Acquisition). *See also* Dual
      Language sketchnote; language acquisition
   icons, 38
   journal prompts, 115–116
   overview, 107
   plotline of story, 108–111
   podcasts, 113–114
   read-alouds, 114
   readers and writers workshop, 111–112
ELL students, 26
Empathy Interview-Understand Your User, *12-11*
environments, drawing, 41
erosion sketchnote, 91
evaluation. *See* assessment and evaluation
Evolution sketchnote, 90
expectations, setting for note taking, 138
exposition, ELA (English Language Acquisition), 108
eyebrows, drawing, 39

F

face shapes, exploring, 44
Face Matrix, 39, 42
Facilitator Standard, 24
falling action, ELA (English Language Acquisition), 108
feedback
   getting, 144
   from structure/partner work, 138
Fletcher, Graham, 127
flipbook option, 52
focus/categorization/synthesis, 32
fonts
   choosing, 47
   choosing for real-time sketchnotes, 73
   video, 48
Food Trucks sketchnote, 141
formula and current content, math class, 130–131
Free Your Fears sketchnote, 143

G

Genius Hour Project Timeline, *12-5*
The Girl Who Thought in Pictures, 21
"The Giver," 108
"glance media," 18
goals and objectives, identifying for real time, 73
Google AI and Quick, Draw!, 13
grading students, 135, 137–138

Grandin, Temple, 21
graphic, building visual vocabulary, 9–13
Graphic Jam activity, 9–13, 68
graphic recording
   5th wave of, 6–7
   origin of, 7
   versus sketchnotes, 7
graphs, using with text, 32
Grey method, 42
group system, creating, 30
groups, students working in, 98, 112. *See also*
      partner work

H

hair styles, exploring, 44
Hamlet, Act 1, Scene 5, 35
handwriting, choosing, 47
Hashtags to Follow and Use sketchnote, 146
hatching and shadows, using, 43
headers, creating, 52
hearing, retention, 20
Herrera, Manuel S., *12-12, 12-13*
hexagon sketchnote, 129
hierarchy of sketchnotes, 46–47, 50
High School Success sketchnote, 102
highlighting and annotating, 68–69, 93, 107
house, drawing, 37
How to Change the World, 79
How Would You Change the World?, 78
Hoxie, Heather, 118–119
human figures, drawing, 41–42

I

"I am different not less," 21
icons. *See also* symbols
   drawing, 10–12, 38
   using with text, 32
ideas, connecting, 49, 73
illustrations, using with text, 32. *See also* drawing
Illustrator Draw app, 60
images
   drawing, 10–11
   making connections with, 5
   processing, 18
   visual concepts as, 17
improvement, 30
Indonesia, Sulawesi, 5
information
   delivery, 15–16
   organizing, 45

retention, 20
    synthesizing, 56
inquiry-driven learning, *12-4*
Instagram, *doodle and lettering challenges*, 147
interpreting content, 71
interviews, *12-10*
iOS devices, 59
iPad Pro, 59
ISTE (International Society for Technology in
    Education) Standards
    3 Knowledge Constructor, 25
    6 Creative Communicator, 26
    6 Facilitator, 24
    Conference & Expo, 149
    for Educators, 24
    for Students, 25
italicized text, 47

J

Jam activity, 9–13, 68
The Jiggly Origins of Jell-o, 99
journal prompts, ELA (English Language Acquisition),
    115–116

K

Kawaii Faces, 44
kinesthetic learning, 15
Kluesner, Misty, 140–141
Knowledge Constructor Standard, 25
KWL (know, want to know, learned) chart, 68

L

landscapes versus portraits, 45, 58
language acquisition, 6. *See also* Dual Language
    sketchnote; ELA (English Language Acquisition)
laptops, drawing, 40
learners, types, 16
learning. *See also* thinking
    4 steps, 16
    auditory, 15
    kinesthetic, 15
    maximizing, 19
    multisensory/multimodal, 15–16
    visual, 15
lecture cues, 71
lesson planning and creativity, *13-3, 13-4, 13-5*
life, drawing symbol or icon for, 12
line segment sketchnote, 129

listening comprehension strategies, 69–72
listening skills, practicing, 67
listening to speakers, 102
Lowry, Lois, 108

M

magnifying glass, drawing, 37
Math 360, 124
math icons, drawing, 38
math sketchnotes
    3 Act Math, 124
    The Cross Product, 131
    formula and current content, 130–131
    The Mindset Revolution, 132
    overview, 121–123
    story problem, 124–128
    vocab review, 129–130
meetings sketchnote, *13-10*
mental cross references, 17
metacognition, 29–31, 44
Meyer, Dan, 124, 127
The Mindset Revolution, math sketchnote, 132
mini-lessons, 111–112
modeling note taking, 24
modular structure, 45, 50
Molly, photo and drawing, 44
mouths, drawing, 39
Mueller, Pam, 56
Multiply sketchnote, 133
multisensory/multimodal learning, 15–16
My Day, drawing, 45

N

Native Tribes Presentation Notes, social studies, 104
NCTE (National Council of Teachers of English), 23, 27
New Bloom's Taxonomy, *13-3*
Newton's Laws, science class, 89
Nixon, Cynthia, 132–133, 148
nonfiction text features, 32. *See also* text
noses, drawing, 42
note taking. *See also* sketchnotes
    in class, 56
    emphasizing, 15
    historical context, 5–6
    modeling, 24
    setting expectations, 138
    standards, 23
    teaching, 23
notebook paper, drawing, 37

O

objectives and goals, identifying for real time, 73
octagon sketchnote, 129
online challenges and prompts, 143
Oppenheimer, Daniel, 56
organizing information, 45
An Overview of the Brain sketchnote, 140

P

paper
    experimenting with, 58
    orientation, 45, 58
partner work, feedback from, 138. See also groups
Pass the Sketchnote challenge, 147
Passages drawing, 46
PBL (project-based learning), 12-4
Peer Interview–What Is Your Teach Legacy? 12-8
pencil, drawing, 37–38
pencil marker, including in videos, 135
pentagon sketchnote, 129
people, drawing, 39–44
perspective, differences in, 11–12
phone, drawing, 11, 40
Pink, Daniel H., 76
planning meetings, 7
plate tectonics, 91
plotline of story, ELA (English Language Acquisition),
        108–111
podcasts
    ELA (English Language Acquisition), 113–114
    speeding up, 73
    and videos, 118
portraits versus landscapes, 45
pre-reading, practicing, 93–94. See also reading skill
presentations, listening to, 46
problem solving, 29
Procreate app, 59–61
professional development. See Bonus Chapter 13
project design. See Bonus Chapter 12

Q

QR codes
    4 Cs of 21st Century Learning, 75
    10-second timer, 10
    Adobe Illustrator Draw app, 60
    Adonit Pro app, 62
    Apple Pencil, 62
    AWW App, 61
    Brains On! podcast, 118
    conference strategy
    current events, 97
    Doodle Buddy app, 60
    doodle of face, 13-8
    Draw Toast TED Talk, 31
    Draw Your Day, 116–117
    Fletcher, Graham, 127
    Google Quick, Draw! 13
    Grandin, Temple, 21
    How to Change the World, 79
    How Would You Change the World?, 78
    Instagram accounts to follow, 149
    The Jiggly Origins of Jell-o, 99
    journal entries, 116
    lab write-ups, 86
    math prompts, 127
    Meyer, Dan, 127
    National Geographic videos, 118
    online resources, 149
    Procreate app, 61
    project planner, 12-7
    science doodle playlist, 86
    sketchnote basics, 53
    Sketchnote template, 97
    Sketchnotes with Nichole, 63
    Sketchpad app, 61
    Skillshare Course on Procreate, 63
    storytelling videos, 109
    teachingtechnix.com, 133
    template, 97
    Twitter accounts to follow, 149
    typography, 48
    Venn diagrams, 101
    websites and online resources, 149
    WeTransfer's Paper app, 60
    "Why People Believe They Can't Draw" TEDx Talks, 8
    YouTube channels to subscribe to, 149
    Ziteboard app, 62
quotes, choosing fonts for, 47

R

read-alouds, ELA (English Language Acquisition), 114
readers and writers workshop, ELA (English Language
        Acquisition), 111–112
reading skill. See also pre-reading
    retention of information, 20
    teaching, 15
real-time versus revisited sketchnotes, 67–70,
        72–74
Reflect on Past Teacher Challenges sketchnote, 145
reflection, 30

resolution, ELA (English Language Acquisition), 108
retention of information, 20
rising action, ELA (English Language Acquisition), 108
Risk Taker sketchnote, *13-5*
Roam, Dan, 69–70
rock/cave paintings, 6
Rohde, Mike, 6
ruler, drawing, 37

S

science class
    convection currents, 91
    cross-referencing sketchnotes, 83
    end-of-unit review, 88–89
    Evolution, 90
    icons, 38
    lab rules, 87–88
    lab write-ups, 83–86
    Lacrosse, Leah, 90–91
    Law of Super Position, 91
    Newton's Laws, 89
    plate tectonics, 91
    protecting eyes and skin, 87
scribbles, 41
sensory processing capacity, 18
shadows and hatching, using, 43
shapes, combining, 37
sharing sketchnotes, 30, 145
Shaw, Graham, 8
Sheltered Instruction sketchnote, 102
sidebars, using with text, 32
#sketch50 annual challenge, 148–149
#sketchCUE annual challenge, 148
Sketchnote Goals, 148
sketchnotes. See also drawing; note taking
    arrows, 49
    components, 35, 136
    containers and banners, 50–51
    differences in perspective, 11–12
    dividers, 49–50
    explained, 5
    fonts, 47–48
    freeing fears about, 144
    versus graphic recording, 7
    headers, 52
    hierarchy, 46–47
    history, 5–7
    implementing basics, 53
    introducing to classes, 11
    model/template, 136

    personal nature of, 7
    practicing, 149–150
    purpose of, 137, 140
    real-time versus revisited, 67
    requirements, 20
    sharing, 145
    during speeches, 101–102
    structure, 44–46
    uniqueness, 12
    use in education, 6
Sketchnotes with Nichole, 63
Sketcho Frenzy video, 48
Sketchpad app, 59, 61
Skillshare Course on Procreate, 63
skyscraper structure, 45
"Slime Eels Release Mucus on Oregon Highway," 95
social media
    joining challenges, 147
    sharing sketchnotes on, 146
social studies
    cause and effect, 101
    current events, 94–98
    highlighting, 93
    Native Tribes Presentation Notes, 104
    practicing pre-reading, 93–94
    sketchnotes during speeches, 101–102
    timelines, 99–100
    visual vocabulary, 104
Social Studies in BSD drawing, 46
solutions, creating, 30
speakers, listening to, 102
speeches, taking sketchnotes during, 101–102
speed, building during real-time sketchnotes, 72–74
Spillman, Monica, 147
staff meeting strategies, *13-9, 13-10*
standards for note taking, 23
STEAM (Science, Technology, Engineering, Arts, Mathematics), *12-4*
stick figures
    adding accessories, 41–42
    body shapes, 43
    starting with, 41
stickers, using in math class, 124
storytelling, 5, 109
students
    grading, 135
    identifying styles, 57
    ISTE Standards (6 Facilitator), 24
    working in groups, 98
stylii, using, 60–62
Sulawesi, Indonesia, 5

symbols, drawing for *life*, 12. *See also* icons
synthesis/focus/categorization, 32
synthesizing information, 56

T

tadpole, drawing, 41
teaching, note taking, 23
teachingtechnix.com, 133
TEDx Talks, "Why People Believe They Can't Draw," 8
template, using for structure, 45–46
Temple Grandin, 21
Terral, Wanda, 148
text. *See also* nonfiction text features
    comprehending, 15
    versus image processing, 18
thinking. *See also* learning
    about thinking, 23, 29
    different ways of, 21
timelines, social studies, 99–100
titles
    determining in real time, 73
    dividers, 49–50
    fonts, 47
    and note hierarchy, 47
    placement, 45
toast, making, 29–31
Tolnai, Cate, 148
topics
    condensing, 45
    reviewing for real time, 73
touch, combining with vision, 19
touchscreen devices, 59
tree, drawing, 37
types of learners, 16
typography. *See* fonts

V

Venn diagrams, 101
verbal concepts as words, 17
"verbal-visual 'trigger' phrases," 69–70
videos
    including pencil markers in, 135
    and podcasts, 118
Vincent, Tony, 13-8
vision
    combining with touch, 19
    sensory processing capacity, 18

visual alphabet
    creating, 36
    using, 37
visual concepts as images, 17
visual note taking, 6
visual retention, 20
Visual Thinking sketchnote, 12-12
visual vocabulary. *See also* words
    5 Basic Elements, 36
    building, 9–13, 15–16, 95
    social studies, 104
visualization, applying to problem solving, 29
vocabulary, including on slides, 71

W

WeTransfer's Paper app, 59–60
What Classroom Activities or Topics Energize You?
    sketchnote, 143
Who/What/When/Where/Why sketchnotes, 95–96
*A Whole New Mind: Why Right-Brainers Will Rule the
    Future*, 76
"Why People Believe They Can't Draw," TEDx Talks,
    8 words. *See also* visual vocabulary
    drawing icons or images for, 10–12
    school-related, 13
    verbal concepts as, 17
workshop model, ELA (English Language
    Acquisition), 111
World Sketchnote Day, 147–148
writers and readers workshop, ELA (English Language
    Acquisition), 111–112
Writing Common Core State Standard, 28
Wujec, Tom, 29

Y

youth, signifying in drawings, 39–40
YouTube
    8 second rule, 18
    channels to subscribe to, 149
    The Jiggly Origins of Jell-o, 99
    speeding up video, 73

Z

Ziteboard app, 62